Contents

BIBLE

Nuts & Bolts

key Bible topics simply explained

Brian Bailie

First published 2017 by Broncle
www.broncle.com

ISBN-13: 978-1544298702
ISBN-10: 1544298706

For this is how God loved the world:
He gave his one and only Son, so that everyone who
believes in him will not perish but have eternal life.

The words of Jesus Christ
John 3:16 (NLT)

This work is dedicated to you, Reader: to helping you
understand the good message that God has for you

for Bowen

in memory of Chris

with thanks to Sammy

Introduction

There is a particular expression I love in the Bible.

You can find it in the Old Testament book of Ezekiel chapter 3 verse 1, and also at the end of the New Testament in the book of Revelation chapter 10 verse 9

To paraphrase the text, it says: *'eat this book!'*

God doesn't want us to just read the Bible - God wants us to consume it, understand it, and let his word become part of who we are.

If you're like me, you'll want to read the list of ingredients to understand what's in the food you eat. Similarly, if we are going to consume the word of God, it is important that we understand the nuts and bolts of what we are reading.

The explanations are not deep theological explorations - I'm not going to pretend to be that clever. I'm just trying to explain the basic principles of the Bible in the way that I would have liked them explained to me when I was new to it all.

I've used five English translations of the Bible to help you fully understand what it means for you:

King James Version (KJV)
New Living Translation (NLT)
English Standard Version (ESV)
New International Version (NIV)
The Message paraphrased version (MSG)

Each Bible version is identified (in brackets) after each quotation in the text. In each case I have tried to use the Bible version that most clearly explains God's message, trusting that the meaning will be perfectly clear to you.

Amen

Amen is a word you frequently hear in church.

People normally end a prayer or a reading from the Bible with *"Amen,"* but what does it mean?

What are we saying to God when we talk to him and then say, *Amen*?

Yes.

Yes, I solemnly agree with this statement,

or, *Yes,* what I say is God's solemn truth.

When we say Amen, we are stating a solemn *Yes* to God. For example, in the Old Testament book of Deuteronomy chapter 27 you can read how Moses commanded the people to make a series of promises to obey God, and after each promise the people said, *"Amen"* by which they meant, *"Yes. Absolutely"*, because they were making a solemn commitment to keep each of those promises.

Many of the books and letters of the New Testament end with *Amen.* In this context *Amen* means that the writer is sealing what he has written with the solemn declaration that this is the truth: *Yes, what I have written here is the truth of God.*

Amen is also translated into English language versions of the Bible using the words, *Verily*, and *Truly*.

So, a statement that begins, *"Amen, Amen,"* may have been translated as *"Verily, verily,..."* or *"Truly, truly,..."* or *"Very truly I tell you,...."*

The only person in the Bible who uses this double *Amen* at the beginning of a statement is Jesus Christ.

Why did Jesus Christ begin some of his statements with "*Amen, Amen*"?

When we speak the truth of God, or the truth to God, we end with the word Amen, and this is appropriate.

However, Jesus Christ is the Son of God, and God is the God of truth, a fact that the prophet Isaiah emphasizes when he says, '*he who blesses himself in the land shall bless himself by the God of truth, and he who takes an oath in the land shall swear by the God of truth.*'
(Isaiah chapter 65 verse 16 - ESV)

What this means is that when Jesus Christ speaks, he only speaks the truth because he is the Son of God, and he is therefore qualified to begin an important statement with the words, *Amen, Amen,...*

Jesus Christ is quoted as saying, "*Amen, Amen*" at the beginning of several of his statements in the Gospel of John. And by using this double Amen, Jesus is emphasizing the fact that what he is saying is *very important* - so sit up and pay attention.

"*Truly, truly,* [Amen, Amen] *I say to you, whoever hears my word, and believes on him who sent me, has eternal life. He shall not come into judgment, but has passed from death to life.*" (John chapter 5 verse 24 - ESV)

We say *Amen* when we speak the solemn truth **to** God.

We say *Amen* when we speak the solemn truth **of** God.

Angels

Movies and storybooks often depict an angel as a lovely demure person wearing a big white nightdress, and drifting about on a large pair of wings. *Really?*

In the original language of the Old Testament, the word that has been used for *angel*, is the Hebrew word *mal'akê*, which can be translated as *messenger*.

In the original language of the New Testament, the word that has been used for *angel*, is the Greek word *angelus*, which again can be translated as *messenger*.

Angels are messengers of God.

But unlike human messengers of God, (whom we know as Old Testament prophets and New Testament apostles), angels are spiritual beings.

In his letter to the Hebrews, Paul explains that, *'angels are only servants - spirits sent to care for people who will inherit salvation.'*   (Hebrews chapter 1 verse 14 - NLT)

What do angels look like to us?

When angels visit people, they appear to look like humans: *'Don't forget to show hospitality to strangers, for some who have done this have entertained angels without realizing it!'*   (Hebrews chapter 13 verse 2 - NLT)

In chapter 19 of the book of Genesis, the wicked people didn't recognize the angels, and thought that the angels were just ordinary people: *'Two angels came to the entrance of the city of Sodom. Lot was sitting there, and when he saw them, he stood up to meet them. Then he welcomed*

them and bowed with his face to the ground. "My lords," he said, "come to my home to wash your feet, and be my guests for the night. You may then get up early in the morning and be on your way again." "Oh no," they replied. "We'll just spend the night out here in the city square." But Lot insisted, so at last they went home with him. Lot prepared a feast for them, complete with fresh bread made without yeast, and they ate. But before they retired for the night, all the men of Sodom, young and old, came from all over the city and surrounded the house. They shouted to Lot, "Where are the men who came to spend the night with you? Bring them out to us so we can have sex with them!"
(Genesis chapter 19 verses 1 to 5 - NLT)

After the crucifixion and burial of Jesus Christ, Mary Magdalene, Mary the mother of James, and Salome bought some burial spices to anoint the body of Jesus; they went to the tomb where his dead body had been laid. *'When they entered the tomb, they saw a young man clothed in a white robe sitting on the right side. The women were shocked, but the angel said, "Don't be alarmed. You are looking for Jesus of Nazareth, who was crucified. He isn't here! He is risen from the dead! Look, this is where they laid his body. Now go and tell his disciples, including Peter, that Jesus is going ahead of you to Galilee. You will see him there, just as he told you before he died."*
(Mark chapter 16 verses 5 to 7 - NLT)

An angel was sent to free Peter from imprisonment: *'The night before Peter was to be placed on trial, he was asleep, fastened with two chains between two soldiers. Others stood guard at the prison gate. Suddenly, there was a bright light in the cell, and an angel of the Lord stood before Peter. The angel struck him on the side to awaken him and said, "Quick! Get up!" And the chains fell off his wrists. Then the angel told him, "Get dressed and put on your sandals." And he did. "Now put on your coat and follow me," the angel ordered. So Peter left the cell, following the angel. But all the time he thought it was a vision. He didn't realize it was actually happening. They passed the first and second guard posts and came to the iron gate leading to the city, and this opened for them all by itself. So they passed through and started walking down the street, and then the angel suddenly left him. Peter finally came to his senses. "It's really true!" he said. "The Lord has sent his angel and saved me from Herod and from what the Jewish leaders had planned to do to me!"*

(Acts chapter 12 verses 6 to 11 - NLT)

How do angels help people?

When the prophet Elijah was running away from Jezebel, who had threatened to kill him, Elijah *'lay down and slept under the broom tree. But as he was sleeping, an angel touched him and told him, "Get up and eat!" He looked around and there beside his head was some bread baked on hot stones and a jar of water! So he ate and drank and lay down again.*

Then the angel of the LORD came again and touched him and said, "Get up and eat some more, or the journey ahead will be too much for you." So he got up and ate and drank, and the food gave him enough strength to travel forty days and forty nights to Mount Sinai, the mountain of God.'

(1 Kings chapter 19 verses 5 to 8 - NLT)

Daniel was thrown into the den of lions for disobeying the command of the Persian king, Darius. Daniel was a friend of King Darius, but the king had been tricked into sentencing him to this gruesome punishment. *'Very early the next morning, the king got up and hurried out to the lions' den. When he got there, he called out in anguish, "Daniel, servant of the living God! Was your God, whom you serve so faithfully, able to rescue you from the lions?" Daniel answered, "Long live the king! My God sent his angel to shut the lions' mouths so that they would not hurt me, for I have been found innocent in his sight. And I have not wronged you, Your Majesty." The king was over-joyed and ordered that Daniel be lifted from the den. Not a scratch was found on him, for he had trusted in his God. Then the king gave orders to arrest the men who had mali-ciously accused Daniel. He had them thrown into the lions' den, along with their wives and children. The lions leaped on them and tore them apart before they even hit the floor of the den.'*
(Daniel chapter 6 verses 19 to 24 - NLT)

Do people have a guardian angel?

The phrase *Guardian Angel* is not a biblical term, how-ever the Bible tells us that angels actively help, support and protect Christian believers.

'Angels are only servants—spirits sent to care for people who will inherit salvation.'
(Hebrews chapter 1 verse 14 - NLT)

David praises God's love, singing, *'God's angel sets up a circle of protection around us while we pray.'*
(Psalm 34 verse 7 - MSG)

Psalm 91 says: *'If you make the* LORD *your refuge, if you make the Most High your shelter, no evil will conquer you; no plague will come near your home. For he will order his angels to protect you wherever you go. They will hold you up with their hands so you won't even hurt your foot on a stone.'* (Psalm 91 verses 9 to 12 - NLT)

In the Gospel of Matthew, Jesus warns: *"Watch that you don't treat a single one of these childlike believers arrogantly. You realize, don't you, that their personal angels are constantly in touch with my Father in heaven?"*
(Matthew chapter 18 verse 10 - MSG)

How's that!

As a Christian believer, angels don't just help, support and protect you, but they also inform God of your particular circumstances.

What do angels actually look like in heaven?

On earth, angels take the form of humans; but in heaven, angels appear very differently.

There are two types of angels that have been described by people who have had a vision of heaven.

These two types of angels are: cherubim, and seraphim.

Cherubim

In the book of Ezekiel chapter 1, the sky opened up and Ezekiel experienced a vision of heaven: *'I looked: I saw an immense dust storm come from the north, an immense cloud with lightning flashing from it, a huge ball of fire glowing like bronze. Within the fire were what looked like four creatures vibrant with life. Each had the form of a human being, but each also had four faces and four wings.*

7

Their legs were as sturdy and straight as columns, but their feet were hoofed like those of a calf and sparkled from the fire like burnished bronze. On all four sides under their wings they had human hands. All four had both faces and wings, with the wings touching one another. They turned neither one way nor the other; they went straight forward.

Their faces looked like this: In front a human face, on the right side the face of a lion, on the left the face of an ox, and in back the face of an eagle. The wings were spread out with the tips of one pair touching the creature on either side; the other pair of wings covered its body. Each creature went straight ahead. Wherever the spirit went, they went. They didn't turn as they went.

The four creatures looked like a blazing fire, or like fiery torches. Tongues of fire shot back and forth between the creatures, and out of the fire, bolts of lightning. The creatures flashed back and forth like strikes of lightning.'

(Ezekiel chapter 1 verses 4 to 14 - MSG)

Seraphim

Seraphim are described in the book of Isaiah, when the prophet describes seeing the LORD who was, *'sitting on a lofty throne, and the train of his robe filled the Temple. Attending him were mighty seraphim, each having six wings. With two wings they covered their faces, with two they covered their feet, and with two they flew. They were calling out to each other, "Holy, holy, holy is the LORD of Heaven's Armies! The whole earth is filled with his glory!" Their voices shook the Temple to its foundations, and the entire building was filled with smoke.'*

(Isaiah chapter 6 verses 1 to 4 - NLT)

Bad angels

Not all angels are messengers of God.

Satan was a powerful angel of God who rebelled and was cast out of heaven to live on the earth.

Satan was cast out of heaven with all of his angel followers. These angel followers of Satan are commonly known as demons.

Demons are spiritual messengers of Satan, and they are responsible for causing a lot of trouble in the world.

'In the last times some will turn away from the true faith; they will follow deceptive spirits and teachings that come from demons. These people are hypocrites and liars, and their consciences are dead.'

(1 Timothy chapter 4 verses 1 and 2 - NLT)

Mark describes an incident when Jesus had been preaching in the synagogue: when suddenly, *'a man in the synagogue who was possessed by an evil spirit cried out, "Why are you interfering with us, Jesus of Nazareth? Have you come to destroy us? I know who you are—the Holy One of God!" But Jesus reprimanded him. "Be quiet! Come out of the man," he ordered. At that, the evil spirit screamed, threw the man into a convulsion, and then came out of him.'*
(Mark chapter 1 verses 23 to 25 - NLT)

Demons (these angels of Satan) recognize and fear the power of Jesus Christ. *'After sunset the people brought to Jesus all the sick and demon-possessed. The whole town gathered at the door, and Jesus healed many who had various diseases. He also drove out many demons, but he would not let the demons speak because they knew who he was.'* (Mark chapter 1 verses 32 to 34 - NIV)

Heavenly angels are spiritual beings, messengers of God, who appear in human form on earth, and appear in amazing form in heaven.

Christian believers enjoy the knowledge that these heavenly angels are constantly looking out for us on God's behalf.

Apostles

The word *apostle* comes from the Greek word *apostolos* which can be translated as, *envoy* or *messenger*.

Apostolos comes from *apostellien*, which can be translated to mean, *to send out*.

Apostles were people who were personally chosen by Jesus Christ to be his envoys who would send out his good message into the world.

There were twelve apostles chosen by Jesus Christ.

'Jesus went up on a mountainside and called to him those he wanted, and they came to him. He appointed twelve that they might be with him and that he might send them out to preach and to have authority to drive out demons.'
(Mark chapter 3 verses 13 to 15 - NIV)

The names of these twelve apostles are:-

Simon, whom Jesus called **Peter**

James, the son of Zebedee

John, also the son of Zebedee

Andrew

Philip

Bartholomew

Matthew

Thomas

James, the son of Alphaeus

Thaddaeus

Simon the Zealot

and **Judas** Iscariot

And after Jesus Christ had been crucified and returned to heaven, Jesus appeared to **Paul** and appointed him as an apostle too. This amazing event is described in the book of Acts chapter 9. Jesus instructed a man called Ananias to go to Paul to help him, because, *"This man* [Paul] *is my chosen instrument to proclaim my name to the Gentiles and their kings and to the people of Israel."* (Acts chapter 9 verse 15 - NIV)

This is why Paul also calls himself an apostle: because he was a personally appointed envoy of Jesus Christ. Paul introduces himself as an apostle in some of his letters: for example, his letter to the Christian community in Rome begins with the words: *'Paul, a servant of Christ Jesus, called to be an apostle and set apart for the gospel of God'* (Romans chapter 1 verse 1 - NIV)

The apostles are the people whom Jesus Christ appointed to send out his good message into the world, and establish his kingdom on earth.

Paul uses the metaphor of a big building to describe the importance of the apostles, telling the Christian community in Ephesus that, *"you are no longer foreigners and strangers, but fellow citizens with God's people and also members of his household, built on the foundation of the apostles and prophets, with Christ Jesus himself as the chief cornerstone. In him the whole building is joined together and rises to become a holy temple in the Lord."* (Ephesians chapter 2 verses 19 to 21 - NIV)

Baptism

When I think of baptism I think of Namaan.

You can read about Namaan in the Old Testament book of 2 Kings chapter 5.

Namaan was a very powerful man; he was an important general in the army of the King of Syria. But despite his wealth and power, he was suffering from a horrible skin disease that was incurable.

One of his slaves was a young girl who had been captured from the Israelites; this slave girl told Namaan's wife that she knew of a prophet of God called Elisha who could cure his horrible disease. Namaan went to see Elisha, arriving with great pomp and ceremony.

But Elisha didn't even bother to greet the general; instead, he sent one of his servants to tell the great and mighty Namaan to go and wash seven times in the River Jordan.

Namaan was very angry. Elisha had snubbed him, and told him to do something ridiculous: why should he bathe in the River Jordan when he could bathe in far superior rivers back in Syria?

As Namaan was about to storm off back to Syria, one of his servants reasoned with him, arguing that they had come all this way, so why not just dip into the Jordan seven times while you are here? The servant argued that if Elisha had asked Naaman to do something difficult and impressive, he would have done it; but Elisha had asked him to do something very simple: just to wash in the river. So why refuse?

Namaan agreed with his servant's logic; he went down to the river and dipped himself in the Jordan seven times, just as Elisha had instructed him.

And Namaan was cured.

Namaan's skin was regenerated as soft and clean as the skin of a young boy.

Baptism is that simple: it is being immersed into water.

If you really, really wanted to become a Christian, and you were told that you had to sit a difficult examination, fill in application forms, put on your best clothes and be interviewed by a panel of intimidating recruiters, you might think that this sounds like a reasonable condition for being granted eternal life and all the wonderful privileges of being a member of God's family. But you need to understand that Jesus Christ has already done everything for you, Jesus Christ has paid the price, Jesus Christ has made the sacrifice: all you need to do is believe.

God is not asking you to do something difficult: he is asking you to do something very, very simple.

Baptism is a simple act of obedience.

If Namaan had stormed off back to Syria he would never have been cured of his horrible skin disease.

Namaan washed away his disease in the River Jordan; and through our baptism we are demonstrating that our sins have been washed away by the sacrifice that Christ made on our behalf when he was killed on the cross.

Different churches practice different kinds of baptism, from a complete immersion in water, to sprinkling some water over a baby's head. But what does the Bible say about baptism?

In the original language of the Bible, the word used for baptism is *Baptizo*.
Baptizo means *overwhelmed*, or *immersed*: for example, *baptizo* can be used to describe dyeing a woolen fleece.
If you want to dye a fleece properly you need to make sure that it is completely submerged in the dye, every last bit of it; because if you fail to completely submerge it and soak it through, the fleece would be dyed unevenly and insufficiently.
Baptism appears to mean a complete immersion.

When you watch a baptism, you can appreciate how the act of immersion into water symbolizes the burial of your old life, and rebirth into your new life with God.
Paul explains this symbolism clearly when he asks: *"Don't you know that all of us who were baptized into Christ Jesus were baptized into his death? We were therefore buried with him through baptism into death in order that, just as Christ was raised from the dead through the glory of the Father, we too may live a new life.*
For if we have been united with him in a death like his, we will certainly also be united with him in a resurrection like his. For we know that our old self was crucified with him so that the body ruled by sin might be done away with, that we should no longer be slaves to sin - because anyone who has died has been set free from sin."
(Romans chapter 6 verses 3 to 7 - NIV)

If you think that baptism isn't so important, if you think that you can get along okay as a Christian without the need to be baptized, in the Gospel of Matthew chapter 3, we are told how Jesus arrived at the River Jordan to be baptized by John the Baptist.

Jesus was baptized. I am definitely not a better person than Jesus. If Jesus was baptized, then I need to be obedient to God's instructions and be baptized too.

When Jesus asked John the Baptist to baptize him, John argued that it should be Jesus who should be baptizing him. But Jesus replied, "*Let it be so now; it is proper for us to do this to fulfill all righteousness.*"
(Matthew chapter 3 verse 15 - NIV)

Baptism does not make you holy.

Baptism does not save you from your sins.

Baptism does not give you supernatural powers.

Baptism demonstrates your sincere obedience to God.

The Birth of Jesus Christ

I hate to burst your bubble, but Santa Claus doesn't have anything to do with the Christmas story.

Before I start the real Christmas story, let me explain who Santa Claus was.

Santa Claus is a translation of the name Saint [Santa] Nicholas [Claus].

Nicholas was a Christian who was born over 200 years *after* the birth of Jesus Christ.

Nicholas didn't keep pet reindeers or live at the North Pole; in truth, Nicholas lived in an area that is near the Mediterranean south coast of modern-day Turkey.

As an active Christian and an important person in the church, Nicholas helped lots of people; but the good deed he is best remembered for is the help he provided to a poor man who had three daughters.

Apparently this man was so poor that he couldn't afford to provide a dowry for his daughters, (a dowry is property or money that a bride brings into her marriage), and this meant that his daughters could never get married. In the culture of those times an unmarried woman had a very bad reputation - his daughters would be ruined.

Nicholas resolved to help the poor man; but it would have been humiliating for him if Nicholas simply gave him a bag of money; so Nicholas cleverly filled three purses with gold coins, one for each daughter, and secretly dropped the purses down the poor man's chimney late at night when the fire was out and everyone was asleep.

However, so the story goes, the poor man had hung up his stockings to dry over the warm embers of the fire, and when Nicholas dropped the purses down the chimney, the purses landed inside the stockings.

You can see how this story about Nicholas has been elaborated to make it look like Santa Claus comes down the chimney and fills your Christmas stocking.

Unfortunately, despite the good Christian legacy of Nicholas, his modern representation as Santa Claus has nothing to do with Biblical teaching, and everything to do with the worldly exploitation of Christmas with modern sales and marketing techniques.

What is Christmas really about?

Perhaps the most astounding book in the whole Bible is also one of the most familiar: the first book of the New Testament, the Gospel of Matthew.

Why?

Well, reading the Bible from the start, and having ploughed your way right through to the end of the Old Testament, when you turn the page and start to read the Gospel of Matthew, you realize that the promises and prophesies of the Old Testament are being fulfilled. Over and over again, Matthew explains how one prophesy after another is being fulfilled by Jesus Christ.

Jesus Christ is undoubtedly the fulfillment of God's promises and the Old Testament prophesies. God's promise to send a Savior is truly realized in Jesus Christ.

The arrival of Christ is prophesied many, many times in the Old Testament, such as here in the book of Isaiah, when the prophet states that, *'the LORD himself will give you a sign: The virgin will conceive and give birth to a son, and call him Immanuel.'* (Isaiah chapter 7 verse 14 - NIV)

Isaiah made this prophesy almost 700 years before the birth of Christ.

Immanuel means *'God with us'*. This is a title, it is not a given name. Isaiah also prophesied that Jesus, *'will be called Wonderful Counselor, Mighty God, Everlasting Father, Prince of Peace.'* (Isaiah chapter 9 verse 6 - NIV)

Jesus Christ is the Son of God

The Son of God did not begin life as the little baby Jesus who was born that night in Bethlehem. The Son of God appeared on earth in human form as the little baby Jesus, adopting the form of a human to live among us; however, the Son of God already existed before being conceived as a human by his mother Mary.

Jesus Christ plainly states: *"Truly, truly, I say to you, before Abraham was, I AM."* (John chapter 8 verse 58 - ESV) Abraham lived about 1,900 years before the time of Jesus.

'In the beginning the Word already existed. The Word was with God, and the Word was God He existed in the beginning with God. God created everything through him, and nothing was created except through him.'
(John chapter 1 verses 1 to 3 - NLT)

Here, the Word, with a capital 'W' is referring directly to the Son of God, Christ.

'The Word became human and made his home among us. He was full of unfailing love and faithfulness. And we have seen his glory, the glory of the Father's one and only Son.'
(John chapter 1 verse 14 - NLT).

This clearly explains that the Son of God existed with his Father from the very beginning of forever; the Son of God became flesh, born on earth as a human, and lived among us. The Son of God made this transformation into human form because he was fulfilling the prophesies of the Old Testament.

Christmas is about the arrival on earth of the Son of God in human form. He had to live among us in human form to fulfill his purpose - he could not have fulfilled his purpose in spiritual form, which is why he was born as the baby Jesus.

The birth of Jesus is about the fulfillment of God's promises to send a Savior to save us from our sins.

What are the facts about the birth of Jesus?

Perhaps you have been to a nativity play at school, or seen a nativity scene illustrated on a Christmas card that shows the little baby Jesus in a stable with Mary and Joseph, a bunch of shepherds, three wise men, and a big star in the night sky?

You can read two accounts of the birth of Jesus: one in the Gospel of Matthew chapters 1 and 2; and another similar account in the Gospel of Luke chapters 1 and 2.

Mary was betrothed to be married to Joseph.

In our society you might compare a betrothal to being engaged to be married; however, in the culture of those times a betrothal was a much more formal commitment to marriage. Mary and Joseph were committed as a couple, but they had not slept together as a married couple - this would come later, after a ceremony, and after the birth of Jesus.

Mary had become pregnant. But she had not become pregnant by a man: Mary had conceived Jesus Christ by the Holy Spirit: by God.

This is what makes Jesus so special.

This is what makes Jesus, the Christ.

The angel Gabriel visited Mary to deliver a personal message from God: *"You will conceive and give birth to a son, and you are to call him Jesus. He will be great and will be called the Son of the Most High. The Lord God will give him the throne of his father David, and he will reign over Jacob's descendants forever; his kingdom will never end."* (Luke chapter 1 verses 31 to 33 - NIV)

As you might expect, Joseph was not impressed by his betrothed wife's pregnancy, and he planned to quietly end their marriage because of this.

However, God hadn't just chosen Mary as the necessary mother to Jesus; God had specifically chosen Joseph to be the earthly father to Jesus.

An angel appeared to Joseph in a dream, and told him: *"Joseph son of David, do not be afraid to take Mary home as your wife, because what is conceived in her is from the Holy Spirit. She will give birth to a son, and you are to give him the name Jesus, because he will save his people from their sins."* (Matthew chapter 1 verses 20 and 21 - NIV)

Joseph son of David?

Joseph's father wasn't called David, but what is meant here is that Joseph's direct ancestor was King David, (the David who killed Goliath the giant about 1,060

years earlier); God had told David: *'I will raise up one of your descendants, your own offspring, and I will make his kingdom strong. He is the one who will build a house—a temple—for my name. And I will secure his royal throne forever. I will be his father, and he will be my son.'*
(2 Samuel chapter 7 verses 12 to 14 - NIV)

The other important point here is that Joseph, through David, is a direct descendant of Abraham, and God had said that, *"all nations on earth will be blessed through him [Abraham]"* (Genesis chapter 18 verse 18 - NIV)

What this means is that both these promises that God had made in the Old Testament are being fulfilled.

While Mary and Joseph were coming to terms with what was happening to them, the ruling Roman authorities had ordered a census to be taken of the population: everyone was ordered to return to their ancestral hometown to be counted.

Joseph was a descendant of David, so he traveled with his betrothed wife to the little town of Bethlehem in Galilee where his ancestor David had originally lived.

Mary was heavily pregnant by the time they reached Bethlehem; and, *'while they were there, the time came for her to give birth. And she gave birth to her firstborn son and wrapped him in swaddling cloths and laid him in a manger, because there was no place for them in the inn.'*
(Luke chapter 2 verses 6 and 7 - NIV) A manger is an open container that animals eat hay from, and which happens to be about the right size and shape for a makeshift cradle for a baby.

Nearby that same night, an angel appeared to some

shepherds who were keeping watch over their sheep.

As you might expect, the shepherds were filled with fear when they saw the brightness shining all around them as the angel appeared.

The angel announced the birth of the Savior to the shepherds, and told them where they would find the baby. Then suddenly, *'there was with the angel a multitude of the heavenly host praising God and saying, "Glory to God in the highest, and on earth peace among those with whom he is pleased!"'* (Luke chapter 2 verses 13 and 14 - ESV)

Without a doubt, this was the arrival of God's gift to the world: a Savior, through whom our sins could be forgiven, through whom we could be made acceptable to God.

After Jesus was born, a group of scholars arrived from the East. These wise men had seen a particular star rise that had indicated the birth of a new king, and they had travelled all this way just to worship him.

King Herod heard about these wise men and their search for the new king; Herod was naturally worried, because he did not want any competition for his throne. So Herod assembled his chief priests and asked them where this new king was to be born: from the old prophesies, the chief priests were able to tell Herod that the new king would be born in Bethlehem.

Herod was very cunning: he sent the wise men to Bethlehem to find the new king, explaining that he also would like to meet and worship him; but it was just a wicked plan to discover the location of this new king, and have him killed.

The star that had told them of the birth of this new king, guided the scholars to the house where they saw Jesus with his mother. They worshiped Jesus, recognizing him as the new King.

They gave Jesus valuable gifts that were appropriate to give to a king: gifts of gold and frankincense and myrrh.

The scholars did not return to Herod to tell him where Jesus was, because they had been warned in a dream that Herod was planning to kill Jesus; the scholars took another route to return to their home in the East.

The Bible doesn't say how many wise men visited Jesus. They brought three gifts, so it is possible that the Christmas cards are correct, and that there were only three of them.

The Bible doesn't say how old Jesus was when the wise men arrived; the Bible simply refers to Jesus as a child, not a baby.

The story also says that they found Jesus living with his mother in a house, not a stable.

At this point the story becomes very distressing.

Herod was very angry when he realized that the scholars from the East had purposely avoided telling him where Jesus was.

An angel appeared to Joseph, the adopting father of Jesus; the angel told Joseph to, *"take the child and his mother and escape to Egypt. Stay there until I tell you, because Herod is going to search for the child to kill him."* (Matthew chapter 2 verse 13 - NIV)

Sure enough, after Mary and Joseph had escaped to

Egypt with Jesus, Herod ordered the execution of every boy aged up to two years old living in Bethlehem and the surrounding area.

The killing of all these innocent little boys sounds terrible, but even this mass murder was prophesied in the Old Testament. God knew what was going to happen, and he protected his Son, because Jesus had a very special purpose to fulfill.

Jesus Christ, the Son of God, had arrived in human form to live among us, to deliver God's new promise.

God's new promise allowed for the inclusion of everyone into God's family, and only the sacrifice of his Son's life would make this possible.

Jesus Christ would die on the cross, accepting the punishment that you and I deserve for our sins; the death of Jesus would be the perfect sacrifice that God needed to forgive our sins.

When you ask God to forgive your sins, God can forgive you because Jesus Christ has already accepted the punishment for your sins when he was crucified.

Christmas has become a frenzied festival of overindulgence: giving and receiving gifts has lost its meaning

The best gift that you can receive is God's forgiveness.

And this forgiveness was only made possible by the gift that God gave us. *"For God so loved the world that he gave his one and only Son, that whoever believes in him shall not perish but have eternal life. God did not send his Son into the world to condemn the world, but to save the world through him."* (John chapter 3 verses 16 and 17 - NIV)

Church

Many people confuse the word *church* to mean a big building where people meet to worship God.

Actually, the definition and use of the word *church* is more confusing than you might think.

The word *church* comes from the Greek word *kuriakos*, which can be translated as, *belonging to the LORD*.

However, the word that is used in the original language of the Bible, which has been translated as *church*, is not *kuriakos*, it is *ecclesia*.

Ecclesia can be translated as the *called-out* people.

The word *ecclesia* was used in Greek society hundreds of years before the beginning of the first Christian communities; *ecclesia* was used to identify a body of elected people who had been chosen, or called out, for public service.

Ecclesia originally had nothing to do with religion.

Some people who translated the Bible into English used the word *church* to replace the word *ecclesia*.

(Some early English translations of the Bible do not use the word *church*.)

English translators of the Bible replaced the word *ecclesia* with the word *church* to identify the people who had been *called out* from the Roman and Jewish systems of the day, and who professed that they now *belong to the Lord*.

The word *church* in our English translations of the Bible identifies these groups of people as living independently from the rule of kings and governments; these groups of people were ruled by God's Holy Spirit, and served Jesus Christ, not the Roman Emperor, (which is one of the reasons why the early Christians were persecuted by the ruling Roman authorities).

What this all means is that the modern biblical use of the word *church* represents a body of people who accept God as the ultimate authority: they do not accept civil government as the ultimate authority.

If we can scrape through all this translation business, the key point is that a church is not a building, nor is it an organization (like the Roman Catholic Church, or the Anglican Church, or Presbyterian Church, or whatever).

A church is a body of people who have accepted Christ as their Savior, and who respond to the teachings of the Bible.

Regularly attending church services does not make you a Christian. Giving generously to support church funds does not make you a Christian. Contributing to church activities and meetings and events does not make you a Christian.

You are a Christian when you believe in the gift of salvation that was achieved for you by the sacrifice that Jesus Christ made when he died for you on the cross: by this sacrifice God can forgive your sins.

However, regularly meeting with fellow Christians is healthy. Church is a family of Christians, and it is good to be an active participant of that family: actively contributing to the health and welfare and growth of the family, caring for each other as brothers and sisters, sharing in sorrows, sharing in joy, praying together and maturing in Christian understanding together.

'Let us not neglect our meeting together, as some people do, but encourage one another, especially now that the day of his [Christ's] return is drawing near.'
(Hebrews chapter 10 verse 25 - NLT)

Paul describes the wider community of Christians in terms of a temple erected to the glory of God:

'This kingdom of faith is now your home country. You are no longer strangers or outsiders. You belong here, with as much right to the name Christian as anyone.

God is building a home. He's using us all—irrespective of how we got here—in what he is building. He used the apostles and prophets for the foundation. Now he's using you, fitting you in brick by brick, stone by stone, with Christ Jesus as the cornerstone that holds all the parts together. We see it taking shape day after day—a holy temple built by God, all of us built into it, a temple in which God is quite at home.' (Ephesians chapter 2 verses 19 to 22 - MSG)

The church is the body of Christ

'Now you are the body of Christ and individually members of it.' (1 Corinthians chapter 12 verse 27 - ESV)

The church is the living body of Christ here on earth.

'The human body has many parts, but the many parts make up one whole body. So it is with the body of Christ. Some of us are Jews, some are Gentiles, some are slaves, and some are free. But we have all been baptized into one body by one Spirit, and we all share the same Spirit.

But our bodies have many parts, and God has put each part

just where he wants it. How strange a body would be if it had only one part! Yes, there are many parts, but only one body. The eye can never say to the hand, "I don't need you." The head can't say to the feet, "I don't need you."

(1 Corinthians chapter 12 verses 12 and 13, 18 to 21 - NLT)

In the same way in which each part is essential to the health and full functionality of a whole human body, so it is with the church: Each church member is essential to the health and full functionality of the church, the body of Christ.

You may have a highly visible role or responsibility to perform within the church, or you may have a simple or unnoticed role: whatever role you perform, be aware that you are essential to the overall effectiveness of the work of the church.

The church is the body of Christian believers who gather under the Fathership of God.

And the church is the living embodiment of Jesus Christ, which is active in the world, working as a united body in the service of God.

'We will speak the truth in love, growing in every way more and more like Christ, who is the head of his body, the church. He makes the whole body fit together perfectly. As each part does its own special work, it helps the other parts grow, so that the whole body is healthy and growing and full of love.'

(Ephesians chapter 4 verses 15 and 16 - NLT)

Circumcision

This was a sensitive subject of great significance to the early Christians; they relied on Paul's enlightened wisdom to clarify the matter.

Men are born with a protective hood of skin that covers the end of their penis; circumcision is the removal of this loose skin so that the end is left permanently exposed. In some cultures circumcision is still practiced, traditionally performed on baby boys at eight days old.

About 1,900 years before the birth of Christ, God made a covenant with Abraham. God told Abraham that he would make him the ancestor of many, many people, and that the whole land of Canaan would be an everlasting possession to Abraham's descendants.

God told Abraham that, *"Every male among you shall be circumcised. You are to undergo circumcision, and it will be the sign of the covenant between me and you."*
(Genesis chapter 17 verses 10 and 11 - NIV)

However, the New Testament delivers a new covenant, and a completely new relationship with God. Circumcision had been practiced by God's chosen people ever since the time of Abraham; but Jesus Christ changed all that.

People no longer needed to be Jewish to be God's chosen people: now anyone could become one of God's chosen people when they asked God for forgiveness; the sacrifice that Jesus Christ made on the cross has allowed God to forgive our sins.

The Jewish converts to Christianity were already circumcised when they were babies; when non-Jews became Christians the Jewish converts demanded that these non-Jewish converts should also be circumcised.

They thought they had a reasonable argument, but Paul made everything perfectly clear: *'For in Christ Jesus neither circumcision nor uncircumcision has any value. The only thing that counts is faith expressing itself through love.'* (Galatians chapter 5 verse 6 - NIV)

If you are a male Christian: relax.

You do not need to be circumcised.

We are not identified as children of God by a physical change that we make to our body: we are identified as children of God by the change in our heart.

Jesus Christ was sacrificed so that we can all be included in God's family; if we could include ourselves in God's family simply by cutting off a little skin, it would mean that Christ's sacrifice was meaningless.

'When you came to Christ, you were "circumcised," but not by a physical procedure. Christ performed a spiritual circumcision—the cutting away of your sinful nature.
For you were buried with Christ when you were baptized. And with him you were raised to new life because you trusted the mighty power of God, who raised Christ from the dead.'
(Colossians chapter 2 verses 11 and 12 - NLT)

Creation

This is a tricky subject for many Christians, because we are educated at school and in the media about evolution and a natural earth history that appears to conflict with the Biblical description.

Genesis chapter 1 verse 1 tells us that God made everything: everything on earth, and everything in the universe: *'In the beginning God created the heavens and the earth'* (KJV)

It's quite simple when you think about it: either everything, absolutely everything including you and me, has been created by an infinite series of random coincidences, (which scientists call evolution); or everything, absolutely everything including you and me, have been created by intelligent design: by God.

From a skeptical point of view, one theory is as incredibly amazing as the other.

Let me describe it in another way: -

Imagine a huge factory, the biggest factory your mind can think of. Now visualize this factory manufacturing a never ending supply of perfectly made objects; objects of infinite intricacy and engineering perfection; objects of an infinite number of designs; designs of every size and shape and form. This factory manufactures continuously, all day, every day, without ceasing.

Can you imagine it?

Now, what if I told you that this factory had no workers, no managers, and no owners.

It sounds completely unbelievable, doesn't it?

But there's more: imagine that this amazing automatic factory was built completely by accident; imagine that this factory that manufactures all these amazing, perfect, and intricately engineered objects, came into existence by an infinite series of random coincidences.

It sounds utterly ridiculous.

It's like suggesting that a complicated mechanical wristwatch is made by putting the hundreds of tiny little parts into a box, and giving it all a really good shake until it forms into an accurately functioning wristwatch.

By comparison, the concept of God creating everything by intelligent design is not so hard to believe.

All the scientists in the world still cannot prove that God is not the creator. Believe me, many, many brilliant scientists have tried to prove that God does not exist, but not one of them has succeeded.

Maybe creation began with a big bang, as some scientists now believe; well, if there was a big bang, it must have been God's big bang.

Okay, so what about evolution?

Evolution is not so difficult to explain; Charles Darwin called it *natural selection*; in simple terms it is the *survival of the fittest*.

Survival of the fittest explains how some living things have adapted over multiple generations to suit their environment.

For example, it explains why the finches on one island have blunt beaks, and very similar finches on the next island have hooked beaks: it's because one island has no nuts but lots of berries; and the other island has no berries but lots of nuts. The breeding of successive generations of finches on each island slowly develops so that only finches with hooked beaks are born on the nutty island, and only finches with blunt beaks are born on the berry island.

The survival of the fittest explains how all living things have survived and adapted to their particular environment, suffering ups and downs, struggles and plagues, disasters and diseases: because the less able ones do not survive, and the more adaptable ones thrive.

Natural selection does not mean that we have evolved from pond slime and tadpoles, (which is theorizing things to extreme lengths to try to convince ourselves that God doesn't exist).

A hummingbird was created as a hummingbird.

An elephant was created as an elephant.

And humans were created as humans.

Survival of the fittest simply means that things living now are the direct result of their predecessors' health, adaptability, stamina and fertility.

And there's nothing biblically contradictory or difficult to believe about that.

'Then God said, "Let the waters swarm with fish and other life. Let the skies be filled with birds of every kind." So God created great sea creatures and every living thing that scurries and swarms in the water, and every sort of bird— each producing offspring of the same kind. And God saw that it was good.'   (Genesis chapter 1 verses 20 and 21 - NLT)

How can you explain a creation that only took six days when you pick up a fossil imbedded in a rock that is clearly very, very ancient?

'On the seventh day God had finished his work of creation, so he rested from all his work.' (Genesis chapter 2 verse 2 NLT)

There are experts who believe that between Genesis chapter 1 verse 1, and verse 3, there was a gap. They argue that this gap may have been millions or billions of years in time; there are others who would argue that these six days of the creation may not have been the 24-hour days that we know today, but may have been six days of immense length.

I am certainly not an expert.

I cannot explain creation; if I attempted to explain creation, I know that I would fail. I was not present at the creation - no one was, except the Creator.

The Bible doesn't provide us with details for the very simple reason that we don't need to know - *we really don't need to know*.

Let me put it in a nutshell: -

Moses wrote the book of Genesis some considerable time after those busy six days of God's creation.

Imagine if God had explained to Moses all about how creation was achieved: the book of Genesis would be absolutely the biggest book ever written, (Moses couldn't possibly have lived long enough to write it all down). Imagine all the science, all the chemistry, all the biology, and physics and mathematics and astronomy and geology and everything else; a book that explained creation could easily fill all the shelves in all the libraries in all the world.

Instead of giving us all that information (which most people simply wouldn't have the mental capacity to understand), Moses gave us all the information we need to know: Genesis chapter 1 verse 1, the very first sentence in the Bible: *'In the beginning God created the heavens and the earth.'* (KJV)

The Crucifixion

Jesus knew that he would eventually be killed.

His execution was a key reason for his existence.

Jesus Christ lived to die.

Jesus Christ died so that you can live.

Why did Jesus Christ need to be killed?

Jesus Christ needed to be killed because God required a perfect sacrifice that would allow him to forgive the sins of the world.

Jesus Christ, the Son of God, was that sacrifice.

'But God showed his great love for us by sending Christ to die for us while we were still sinners.'

(Romans chapter 5 verse 8 - NLT)

Jesus Christ died for you and me, so that our sins can be forgiven, because when our sins are forgiven we are made acceptable to God.

Why did God need a sacrifice?

Near the beginning of the Bible, in Genesis chapter 3, sin entered the world.

The serpent had deceived Eve in the Garden of Eden.

Eve took the fruit from the Tree of the Knowledge of Good and Evil, (the very tree from which God had forbidden Adam to eat), and Adam and Eve both ate the fruit.

The serpent is identified in the book of Revelation as, *'that ancient serpent, who is called the devil and Satan, the deceiver of the whole world.'*

(Revelation chapter 12 verse 9 - ESV)

As soon as sin had entered the world, God had a plan.

In the Garden of Eden, God told the serpent: *"I will put enmity between you and the woman, and between your offspring and hers; he will crush your head, and you will strike his heel."* (Genesis chapter 3 verse 15 - NIV)

The offspring of the woman, who would eventually crush the serpent's head, is Jesus Christ.

God's plan to fix sin was to send his Son as the perfect sacrifice that allowed God to forgive our sins.

Through the sacrifice of Jesus Christ, sin would be defeated.

Throughout the Old Testament, the only way that God's chosen people could make themselves acceptable to God was through their obedience to the strict laws that God had given to Moses.

These strict laws included circumcision, not eating meat from animals that were considered unclean, performing rituals, and offering sacrifices of animals.

God's chosen people could only achieve God's satisfaction by remaining obedient to these strict laws.

But remaining obedient proved to be too difficult, which meant that the people had to continually sacrifice animals to earn continual forgiveness from God for their continual disobedience.

What was needed was a special and perfect sacrifice that would be the sacrifice to end all sacrifices.

God loves us so much that he gave his only Son as this very special and perfect sacrifice.

'God showed how much he loved us by sending his one and

only Son into the world so that we might have eternal life through him. This is real love—not that we loved God, but that he loved us and sent his Son as a sacrifice to take away our sins.'   (1 John chapter 4 verse 10 - NLT)

By the sacrifice of God's only Son, the sins of everyone can be forgiven.

People would no longer need to earn forgiveness through animal sacrifice.

Because of the sacrifice that Jesus Christ made when he was killed on the cross, you and I can freely accept God's forgiveness of our sins.

We do not earn God's forgiveness.

We receive forgiveness as a gift from God.

'Under the old system, the blood of goats and bulls and the ashes of a heifer could cleanse people's bodies from ceremonial impurity. Just think how much more the blood of Christ will purify our consciences from sinful deeds so that we can worship the living God. For by the power of the eternal Spirit, Christ offered himself to God as a perfect sacrifice for our sins. That is why he is the one who mediates a new covenant between God and people, so that all who are called can receive the eternal inheritance God has promised them. For Christ died to set them free from the penalty of the sins they had committed under that first covenant.'   (Hebrews chapter 9 verses 13 to 14 - NLT)

Because sin needed to be defeated, Jesus Christ allowed himself to be sacrificed.

The death of Jesus Christ has allowed God to forgive the sins of everyone who believes.

'We are made right with God by placing our faith in Jesus Christ. And this is true for everyone who believes, no matter who we are. For everyone has sinned; we all fall short of God's glorious standard. Yet God, in his grace, freely makes us right in his sight. He did this through Christ Jesus when he freed us from the penalty for our sins.'
(Romans chapter 3 verses 22 to 24 - NLT)

When you realize that you are a sinner, when you realize that your standards will always fail to meet the standards of perfection required by God, and when you believe that God gave his only Son as the perfect sacrifice that allows him to forgive your sins: you achieve God's forgiveness.

All you need to do is: ask God.

'If you declare with your mouth, "Jesus is Lord," and believe in your heart that God raised him from the dead, you will be saved. For it is with your heart that you believe and are justified, and it is with your mouth that you profess your faith and are saved.'
(Romans chapter 10 verses 10 and 11 - NIV)

The Son of God appeared on earth in human form as the person, Jesus Christ. To fulfill his purpose as a holy sacrifice, Jesus Christ needed to be killed.

Jesus upset the religious establishment so much that they actively wanted to kill him, and they conspired to have him arrested: his execution became inevitable.
When Jesus Christ was killed, God's promises and the Old Testament prophecies would be fulfilled, and the opportunity of salvation for all would be realized.

Why did the religious leaders want to kill Jesus?

There are several reasons: -

Jesus claimed to be the Messiah, and was performing miracles: Jesus raised his friend Lazarus from death; *'Many of the people who were with Mary* [the sister of Lazarus] *believed in Jesus when they saw this happen. But some went to the Pharisees and told them what Jesus had done. Then the leading priests and Pharisees called the high council together. "What are we going to do?" they asked each other. "This man certainly performs many miraculous signs. If we allow him to go on like this, soon everyone will believe in him. Then the Roman army will come and destroy both our Temple and our nation."*
(John chapter 11 verses 45 to 48 - NLT)

Jesus had openly condemned the religious leaders: In all of Matthew chapter 23, Jesus criticized the teachers of religious law and the Pharisees, calling them frauds and hypocrites. Jesus declared, *"You're hopeless, you religion scholars and Pharisees! Frauds! You burnish the surface of your cups and bowls so they sparkle in the sun, while the insides are maggoty with your greed and gluttony. Stupid Pharisee! Scour the insides, and then the gleaming surface will mean something."*
(Matthew chapter 23 verses 25 and 26 - MSG)

Jesus was a threat to the established religious system: John described an occasion when, *'Jesus went to Jerusalem. In the Temple area he saw merchants selling cattle, sheep, and doves for sacrifices; he also saw dealers at tables exchanging foreign money. Jesus made a whip from some ropes and chased them all out of the Temple. He drove out*

the sheep and cattle, scattered the money changers' coins over the floor, and turned over their tables. Then, going over to the people who sold doves, he told them, "Get these things out of here. Stop turning my Father's house into a marketplace!"
(John chapter 2 verses 13 to 16 - NLT)

Jesus surrounded himself with common and disreputable people: Jesus shared meals with low-class and anti-social people, *'But when the teachers of religious law who were Pharisees saw him eating with tax collectors and other sinners, they asked his disciples, "Why does he eat with such scum?" When Jesus heard this, he told them, "Healthy people don't need a doctor—sick people do. I have come to call not those who think they are righteous, but those who know they are sinners."*
(Mark chapter 2 verses 16 and 17 - NLT)

Jesus demonstrated a lack of respect for the religious traditions: Mark describes how, *'Jesus went into the synagogue again and noticed a man with a deformed hand. Since it was the Sabbath, Jesus' enemies watched him closely. If he healed the man's hand, they planned to accuse him of working on the Sabbath. Jesus said to the man with the deformed hand, "Come and stand in front of everyone." Then he turned to his critics and asked, "Does the law permit good deeds on the Sabbath, or is it a day for doing evil? Is this a day to save life or to destroy it?" But they wouldn't answer him. He looked around at them angrily and was deeply saddened by their hard hearts. Then he said to the man, "Hold out your hand." So the man held out his hand, and it was restored! At once the Pharisees went away*

and met with the supporters of Herod to plot how to kill Jesus.'
(Mark chapter 3 verses 1 to 6 - NLT)

What were the series of events that led to the execution of Jesus?

The events surrounding the crucifixion of Jesus Christ are described in: -

The Gospel of Matthew chapters 26 and 27

The Gospel of Mark chapters 14 and 15

The Gospel of Luke chapters 22 and 23

And the Gospel of John chapters 13 to 19

Judas Iscariot, (one of the twelve apostles whom Jesus had appointed), was persuaded by the chief priest to betray Jesus; the chief priest had promised to pay a reward of 30 pieces of silver to the person who would secure the arrest of Jesus Christ.

As the time of his betrayal approached, Jesus knew what he was facing.

Jesus told his disciples, *"As you know, Passover begins in two days, and the Son of Man will be handed over to be crucified."*   (Matthew chapter 26 verse 2 - NLT)

Jesus is very deeply apprehensive about his impending crucifixion, and he prayed to his Father: *"Now my soul is deeply troubled. Should I pray, 'Father, save me from this hour'? But this is the very reason I came! Father, bring glory to your name." Then a voice spoke from heaven, saying, "I have already brought glory to my name, and I will do so again." When the crowd heard the voice, some thought it was thunder, while others declared an angel had spoken to him. Then Jesus told them, "The voice was for your benefit, not mine. The time for judging this world has come, when Satan, the ruler of this world, will be cast out. And when I am lifted up from the earth, I will draw everyone to myself."* (John chapter 12 verses 27 to 32 - NLT)

On the first day of the Festival of Unleavened Bread, when the Passover lamb is sacrificed, a Passover meal was prepared in an upper room of a house in Jerusalem for Jesus Christ and his disciples.

Jesus knew that he would be betrayed by his disciple, Judas Iscariot. *'When it was evening, Jesus sat down at the table with the Twelve. While they were eating, he said, "I tell you the truth, one of you will betray me."*
(Matthew chapter 26 verse 20 - NLT)

Jesus identified Judas as the disciple who would betray him: *"It is the one to whom I give the bread I dip in the bowl." And when he had dipped it, he gave it to Judas, son of Simon Iscariot. When Judas had eaten the bread, Satan entered into him. Then Jesus told him, "Hurry and do what you're going to do."* (John chapter 13 verse 27 - NLT)

'As they were eating, Jesus took some bread and blessed it. Then he broke it in pieces and gave it to the disciples, saying, "Take it, for this is my body." And he took a cup of wine and gave thanks to God for it. He gave it to them, and they all drank from it. And he said to them, "This is my blood, which confirms the covenant between God and his people. It is poured out as a sacrifice for many."
(Mark chapter 14 verses 22 to 24 - NLT)

Then Jesus and his disciples sang a hymn, and went out to the Mount of Olives.

At the olive grove called Gethsemane, Jesus prayed alone. Jesus, *'walked away, about a stone's throw, and knelt down and prayed, "Father, if you are willing, please take this cup of suffering away from me. Yet I want your will to be done, not mine." Then an angel from heaven appeared and strengthened him. He prayed more fervently, and he was in such agony of spirit that his sweat fell to the ground like great drops of blood.'*
(Luke chapter 22 verses 41 to 43 - NLT)

Sweating blood demonstrates the extreme anxiety that Jesus Christ was suffering.

Hematidrosis (bloody sweat, to you and me) is a very rare medical condition, which is caused when people are under extreme emotional stress: tiny capillaries in the sweat glands burst and mix with sweat.

Jesus was clearly agonizing about the ordeal that he would soon have to endure.

Judas appeared in the olive grove, leading a crowd.

'The leading priests and Pharisees had given Judas a contingent of Roman soldiers and Temple guards to accompany him. Now with blazing torches, lanterns, and weapons, they arrived at the olive grove. Jesus fully realized all that was going to happen to him, so he stepped forward to meet them. "Who are you looking for?" he asked.'
(John chapter 18 verses 3 to 4 - NLT)

'The traitor, Judas, had given them [the Temple guards] *a prearranged signal: "You will know which one to arrest when I greet him with a kiss." So Judas came straight to*

Jesus. *"Greetings, Rabbi!" he exclaimed and gave him the kiss. Jesus said, "My friend, go ahead and do what you have come for." Then the others grabbed Jesus and arrested him. But one of the men with Jesus pulled out his sword and struck the high priest's slave, slashing off his ear. "Put away your sword," Jesus told him. "Those who use the sword will die by the sword. Don't you realize that I could ask my Father for thousands of angels to protect us, and he would send them instantly? But if I did, how would the Scriptures be fulfilled that describe what must happen now?" Then Jesus said to the crowd, "Am I some dangerous revolutionary, that you come with swords and clubs to arrest me? Why didn't you arrest me in the Temple? I was there teaching every day. But this is all happening to fulfill the words of the prophets as recorded in the Scriptures." At that point, all the disciples deserted him and fled.'*
(Matthew chapter 26 verses 48 to 56 - NLT)

Jesus was arrested and taken to the home of the high priest where the leading priests, the elders and the teachers of religious law had gathered together. They were trying to find evidence against Jesus that would enable them to have him executed.

Accusations were made against Jesus.

'The high priest stood up and said to Jesus, "Well, aren't you going to answer these charges? What do you have to say for yourself?" But Jesus remained silent. Then the high priest said to him, "I demand in the name of the living God—tell us if you are the Messiah, the Son of God." Jesus replied, "You have said it. And in the future you will see the Son of Man seated in the place of power at God's right hand and

coming on the clouds of heaven." Then the high priest tore his clothing to show his horror and said, "Blasphemy! Why do we need other witnesses? You have all heard his blasphemy. What is your verdict?" "Guilty!" they shouted. "He deserves to die!" Then they began to spit in Jesus' face and beat him with their fists. And some slapped him, jeering, "Prophesy to us, you Messiah! Who hit you that time?"
(Matthew chapter 26 verses 62 to 68 - NLT)

The next morning the entire council took Jesus to Pilate, the Roman governor.
They accused Jesus of stirring trouble and of claiming that he is the long awaited Messiah, the king of the Jews.

Pilate could find no fault with Jesus; but when he discovered that Jesus was from Galilee, Pilate sent him to Herod, because Galilee was under the jurisdiction of Herod, and Herod happened to be in Jerusalem at that time.

'Herod was delighted at the opportunity to see Jesus, because he had heard about him and had been hoping for a long time to see him perform a miracle. He asked Jesus question after question, but Jesus refused to answer. Meanwhile, the leading priests and the teachers of religious law stood there shouting their accusations. Then Herod and his soldiers began mocking and ridiculing Jesus. Finally, they put a royal robe on him and sent him back to Pilate.'
(Luke chapter 23 verses 8 to 11 - NLT)

Again, Pilate examined Jesus, and again Pilate could find no reason to find Jesus guilty of any crime that deserved punishment.

A *'mighty roar rose from the crowd, and with one voice they shouted, "Kill him, and release Barabbas to us!" (Barabbas was in prison for taking part in an insurrection in Jerusalem against the government, and for murder.)   Pilate argued with them, because he wanted to release Jesus.   But they kept shouting, "Crucify him! Crucify him!"   For the third time he demanded, "Why? What crime has he committed? I have found no reason to sentence him to death.   So I will have him flogged, and then I will release him."   But the mob shouted louder and louder, demanding that Jesus be crucified, and their voices prevailed.   So Pilate sentenced Jesus to die as they demanded.'*
(Luke chapter 23 verses 18 to 25 - NLT)

The fate of Jesus was sealed: against his intuition, *'Pilate released Barabbas to them.   He ordered Jesus flogged with a lead-tipped whip, then turned him over to the Roman soldiers to be crucified.'*
(Matthew chapter 27 verse 26 - NLT)

'Some of the governor's soldiers took Jesus into their headquarters and called out the entire regiment.   They stripped him and put a scarlet robe on him.   They wove thorn branches into a crown and put it on his head, and they placed a reed stick in his right hand as a scepter.   Then they knelt before him in mockery and taunted, "Hail! King of the Jews!"   And they spit on him and grabbed the stick and struck him on the head with it.
When they were finally tired of mocking him, they took off the robe and put his own clothes on him again.   Then they led him away to be crucified.'
(Matthew chapter 27 verses 27 to 31 - NLT)

The crucifixion of Jesus

I find this very distressing to describe.

Perhaps the image of Jesus hanging on the cross has been so over-used that we have become numbed to the horrific reality of this inhumane form of execution.

By now, Jesus must have been in a truly terrible physical and mental condition.

Having been flogged with a lead-tipped whip, his wounds must have been oozing blood, weakening him and making even the slightest movement agonizing.

The pain of the crown of thorns pressing into his flesh must have been unbearable. (I have held the thorns that grow around Jerusalem; each thorny spike grows perhaps 2½ inches long, and they are very unforgiving against the flesh.)

Because of his weakened and suffering state, a passer-by was instructed to help Jesus carry his cross to the place of execution, a place called Golgotha.

Then the Gospel accounts simply state that Jesus was nailed to the cross. But the act of nailing someone to a wooden beam is unspeakably cruel.

A Roman soldier may have forced his thumb into the palm of Jesus' hand to find the correct position to drive a heavy wrought-iron nail, hammering the spike between the bones in the hand, and deep into the solid timber.

The nail would be hammered in tight against the flesh, ensuring it could support the full weight of a man without stripping out the flesh and tendons between the fingers. And then this cruel, agonizing act would have been repeated on the other hand.

His feet were skewered into place in a similar fashion.

With the knees flexed to allow the feet to be positioned upright against the timber, one foot would have been pressed backwards against the other, and both feet extended downwards. A long, crude wrought-iron nail would have been hammered through the arch of both feet, securing them to the upright timber beam.

The super-sensitive nerves in his hands and feet would have sent agonizing shockwaves exploding through Jesus' brain. And the distress must have been truly unbearable as they raised the cross vertically and slotted it into place with an unforgiving bump.

And then Jesus was left to hang there, helplessly, suspended by his hands and feet. Unable to relieve the searing agony in his hands by supporting himself by his feet. And unable to relieve the excruciating pain in his feet by raising himself by his hands.

Crucifixion is indescribable suffering.

Two criminals were crucified with Jesus, one on either side of him.

'Pilate posted a sign on the cross that read, "Jesus of Nazareth, the King of the Jews." The place where Jesus was crucified was near the city, and the sign was written in Hebrew, Latin, and Greek, so that many people could read it. Then the leading priests objected and said to Pilate, "Change it from 'The King of the Jews' to 'He said, I am King of the Jews.'" Pilate replied, "No, what I have written, I have written." (John chapter 19 verses 19 to 22 - NLT)

Jesus was unclothed when he was hung on the cross. *'When the soldiers had crucified Jesus, they divided his clothes among the four of them. They also took his robe, but it was seamless, woven in one piece from top to bottom. So they said, "Rather than tearing it apart, let's throw dice for it."* (John chapter 19 verses 23 and 24 - NLT)

'Jesus said, "Father, forgive them, for they don't know what they are doing."
And the soldiers gambled for his clothes by throwing dice. The crowd watched and the leaders scoffed.
"He saved others," they said, "let him save himself if he is really God's Messiah, the Chosen One." The soldiers mocked him, too, by offering him a drink of sour wine. They called out to him, "If you are the King of the Jews, save yourself!" (Luke chapter 23 verses 34 to 37 - NLT)

Jesus was nailed to the cross at 9am. At 12noon, darkness fell across the whole land, and it remained dark until 3pm. At about 3pm Jesus called out the opening words of Psalm 22: *"My God, my God, why hast thou forsaken me?"* (KJV)

Psalm 22 is a very emotional psalm of David that prophesies and describes the predicament that Jesus found himself in: scorned, punished and helpless, yet acknowledging God's presence, and praising God's authority and righteousness.

Read Psalm 22 in relation to the crucifixion of Jesus Christ. David wrote this psalm about 1,040 years before the crucifixion of Christ.

Jesus had been hanging in agony, slowly dying on the cross for six hours. And then he died.

'It was the day of preparation, and the Jewish leaders didn't want the bodies hanging there the next day, which was the Sabbath (and a very special Sabbath, because it was Passover week). So they asked Pilate to hasten their deaths by ordering that their legs be broken. Then their bodies could be taken down. So the soldiers came and broke the legs of the two men crucified with Jesus. But when they came to Jesus, they saw that he was already dead, so they didn't break his legs. One of the soldiers, however, pierced his side with a spear, and immediately blood and water flowed out.'
(John chapter 19 verses 31 to 34 - NLT)

As you read the series of events leading up to the arrest of Jesus, you may have noticed several occasions when Jesus could have easily avoided capture: -

Jesus told his disciples that he would be handed over for crucifixion in two days time. Jesus had two days in which he could flee the city and make good his escape.

Jesus knew that Judas was going to betray him; it would have been easy to expose this plot and get the other disciples to stop Judas from betraying him.

In the olive grove at Gethsemane, when Jesus was so stressed that he was sweating blood, it would have been natural instinct to disappear into the night and avoid arrest.

When the Roman governor examined him, Jesus could have argued in defense of the accusations.

Pilate could find no reason to find Jesus guilty and had pleaded for the crowd to be reasonable. Pilate had also ordered the sign hung on the cross with Jesus, which read, *'King of the Jews,'* and had refused to change it to *'He Said I Am King of the Jews.'* Pilate appears to have had more than a little sympathy for Jesus, which Jesus could have easily appealed to, to save himself from execution.

Jesus knew that he was going to be executed.
Jesus knew that his suffering was going to be horrific.
Jesus had several opportunities to avoid his arrest and execution.
But Jesus knew that he must be sacrificed so that God can forgive the sins of the world.

'This is real love—not that we loved God, but that he loved us and sent his Son as a sacrifice to take away our sins.'
(1 John chapter 4 verse 10 - NLT)

'God demonstrates his own love for us in this: While we were still sinners, Christ died for us.'
(Romans chapter 5 verse 8 - NIV)

"God so loved the world, that he gave his only Son, that whoever believes in him should not perish but have eternal life." (John chapter 3 verse 16 - ESV)

Jesus Christ suffered a brutal flogging, humiliation and ridicule, and a horrific and inhumane execution that defies true description.

Jesus suffered all this, for you.
Jesus suffered all this so that you can receive forgiveness from God for all of your sins.

'We praise God for the glorious grace he has poured out on

us who belong to his dear Son. He is so rich in kindness and grace that he purchased our freedom with the blood of his Son and forgave our sins.'
(Ephesians chapter 1 verses 6 and 7 - NLT)

Please read about the Resurrection to understand the implications that the crucifixion of Jesus Christ has for your salvation

Disciples

The word *disciple* comes from the Latin word *discipulus*, which can be translated as, *learner*.

Disciples are students who are taught in a particular doctrine.

When we read the Bible, the word *disciple* is used to describe a person who is learning the truth about God.

Jesus gave his disciples a new command to demonstrate the difference that God's salvation has made in their lives: *"Love one another. As I have loved you, so you must love one another. By this everyone will know that you are my disciples, if you love one another."*
(John chapter 13 verses 34 and 35 - NIV)

The disciples are not just the apostles, (the apostles were the people who were personally chosen by Jesus to be the envoys of his good news to the world).

Disciples are the growing numbers of followers of Christ. Disciples are believers and followers in the way of Christ.

Disciples are Christians.

In the book of Acts chapter 11 verse 26, we are told that, *'The disciples were first called Christians at Antioch.'* There, at the city of Antioch, (located near the southern coast of modern-day Turkey), the disciples are called Christians for the very first time.

If you are a Christian, you are a disciple of Christ.

God

Unfortunately the human mind struggles to comprehend the ultimate holiness, supremacy and perfection of God.

The human mind cannot compute infinity - we don't understand *forever* in the magnitude or dimension in which God exists.

In heaven, God is worshiped continuously. In the book of Revelation, John describes his vision of the heavenly creatures worshiping God, who *'never cease to say, "Holy, holy, holy, is the Lord God Almighty, who was and is, and is to come!"* (Revelation chapter 4 verse 8 - ESV)

In heaven the angels endlessly demonstrate the absolute and supreme holiness and power of God.

Who is God?

In the book of Exodus chapter 3 verse 14, God instructed Moses to deliver a personal message to the Israelites. Moses asked God what he should say if the Israelites ask who the message is from.

God replied, *"I AM Who I AM."*

God told Moses to tell the Israelites that *"I AM has sent me to you."*

For me, this sums up God perfectly: God is the one and only God.

When you read the Old Testament and see the word 'Lord' written in all capital letters as 'LORD', this represents the English translation of God's name from the Hebrew language, which literally means, "I AM".

The Hebrew word that is translated into English as "I AM" is replaced with the word 'LORD' to prevent the possible misuse or abuse of God's name, because God commanded: *"Thou salt not take the name of the LORD thy God in vain; for the LORD will not hold him guiltless that taketh his name in vain."* (Exodus chapter 20 verse 7 - KJV)

How powerful is God?

When God created the heavens and the earth, he didn't roll up his sleeves and get his hands dirty.

God spoke: creation happened.

Look at the book of Genesis chapter 1, verses 3, 6, 9, 11, 14, 20, 24, and 26: all begin with the phrase, *"And God said,..."*

'And God said, "Let there be light", and there was light.' (Genesis chapter 1 verse 3 - KJV)

God is so powerful that he only needs to speak, and creation happens.

What does God look like?

In the book of Exodus, God told Moses that, *"you cannot see my face, for man shall not see me and live."* (Exodus chapter 33 verse 20 - ESV)

The only person who has seen God is his own Son, Jesus Christ. *'No one has ever seen God, except the one and only Son, who is himself God and is in closest relationship with the Father'* (John chapter 1 verse 18 - NLT)

If God is invisible, how can we tell if he exists?

It would be easy to believe in God if he had his own TV show, if you could visit him in his own *Heavenly Land* theme park, or if he was constantly being photographed for popular magazines and newspapers.

But we can believe in lots of things that are invisible: -

You can't see the wind, but you know it exists because you can feel it and see how destructive it can be in a storm.

You can't see the electricity that makes your lights come on, but you know that you could be killed or seriously injured by its power if you were foolish enough to replace a light bulb with your fingers.

And my brother didn't see his lovely big glass door until he ran through it and ended up in a bloody mess on the other side.

I accept that many people have a problem believing in God. However, when you accept Jesus Christ as your Savior, you will know that God exists because he gives you a very special gift.

When you come to know God, God gives you his Holy Spirit. And there is no denying the existence of the Holy Spirit in your life because you immediately realize that something wonderful and peaceful and loving has enveloped you.

'Each of you must repent of your sins and turn to God, and be baptized in the name of Jesus Christ for the forgiveness of your sins. Then you will receive the gift of the Holy Spirit.' (Acts chapter 2 verse 38 - NLT)

In the New Testament Jesus Christ delivers a new covenant, a new promise, and a new relationship between mankind and God.

In the New Testament, Jesus refers to God as Father, but he uses the familiar and respectful term for father, *Abba*, (perhaps the equivalent of our familiar and respectful title, *Papa*).

Not only does Jesus Christ call God, Father, but he authorized and instructed us to do the same when he said, *"Pray like this: Our Father in heaven,..."*
(Matthew chapter 6 verse 9 - ESV)

This new relationship that we can enjoy with God is an enormous privilege.

When you believe in God, and accept the truth that Jesus Christ has paid the penalty for your sins, you become a child of God: God becomes your Father.

God adopts you as his own child.

'You have received the Spirit of adoption as sons, by whom we cry, "Abba! Father"'
(Romans chapter 8 verse 15 - ESV)

Adoption is something that is easy for me to understand, because I was adopted when I was a baby. My natural parents couldn't keep me and raise me, so I was adopted by my mum and dad, who raised me as *their* child. I was given a new name and a new identity, and a whole new life. I enjoyed their unconditional love, and all the privileges that any natural child would expect to receive from their parents.

Adoption is 100% commitment, including inheritance.
'He [God] *has caused us to be born again to a living hope through the resurrection of Jesus Christ from the dead, to an inheritance that is imperishable, undefiled and unfading,...'* (1 Peter chapter 1 verses 3 to 5 - ESV)

What inheritance will God's children enjoy?

'Now we live with great expectation, and we have a priceless inheritance—an inheritance that is kept in heaven for you, pure and undefiled, beyond the reach of change and decay.'
(1 Peter chapter 1 verses 3 and 4 - NLT)

In my Father's house are many mansions: if it were not so, I would have told you. I go to prepare a place for you.
(John chapter 14 verse 2 - KJV)

'Come, you who are blessed by my Father, inherit the kingdom prepared for you...."
(Matthew chapter 25 verses 34 - ESV)

What happens to a Christian who strays away from God?

Does God give up on people who abandon him?
No!
When I [frequently] caused trouble, my adopted mum and dad never gave up on me, they would never dream about disowning me, they'd never think of changing my name back to what it was before they adopted me as their child. My adoptive parents were totally 100% committed to me in every way. And the same thing applies to our relationship with God.

You have probably heard of the parable of the Prodigal Son; you can read this story in the Gospel of Luke chapter 15.
The prodigal son decided that he wanted to experience the world for himself, so he took his inheritance from his father, and off he went.
The son wasted his money on fancy things and having a

good time, but soon the money ran out, and his good-time-friends abandoned him.

Destitute and hungry, the son found himself eating the food thrown out for the pigs; ashamed, he decided to return home to ask his father if he could be accepted back into the family household as a servant.

The son remorsefully said, *"Father, I have sinned against God and against you. I am no longer worthy to be called your son."* (Luke chapter 15 verse 21 - ESV)

The son felt unworthy of his birthright: ashamed, he is content to be one of the servants.

The son was willing to stop being a son.

But the father was not willing to stop being a Father.

'The father said to his servants, "Bring quickly the best robe, and put it on him, and put a ring on his hand, and shoes on his feet. And bring the fattened calf and kill it, and let us eat and celebrate. For this my son was dead, and is alive again; he was lost, and is found."
And they began to celebrate.'
(Luke chapter 15 verses 22 to 24 - ESV)

When we are adopted by God, even though we may give up on him, he will never give up on us.

Paul confirms God's 100% commitment to his adopted children when he writes: *"For I am convinced, that neither death, nor life, nor angels, nor principalities, nor powers, nor things present, nor things to come, nor height, nor depth, nor anything else in all creation, shall be able to separate us from the love of God that is in Christ Jesus our Lord."* (Romans chapter 8 verses 38 and 39 - ESV)

God corrects his children

When you were young, did you ever get chastised by your parents for doing something dangerous, like playing with fire or fooling around near a fast-flowing river? Maybe your father gave you a slap on the back of your legs to reward your foolishness; if so, you'll appreciate how your punishment was intended to make sure you stopped putting yourself at risk - your punishment was intended to protect you.

Similarly, God will chastise his children when they put themselves at risk of condemnation.

When Paul explained how we should examine ourselves before we participate in the Lord's Supper, he delivered a very stern warning: *'If you eat the bread or drink the cup without honoring the body of Christ, you are eating and drinking God's judgment upon yourself. That is why many of you are weak and sick and some have even died.*

But if we would examine ourselves, we would not be judged by God in this way. Yet when we are judged by the Lord, we are being disciplined so that we will not be condemned along with the world.' (1 Corinthians chapter 11 verses 29 to 32 - NLT)

God prevents Christians from participating in the Lord's Supper when they approach this solemn act of remembrance with a carefree or indifferent attitude; through illness and even death, God prevents these irreverent Christians from participating in the Lord's Supper so that they can avoid facing condemnation at the Judgment. This is Fatherly love: God is correcting his children, and preventing them from getting into much deeper trouble later on.

"My child, don't make light of the LORD's discipline, and don't give up when he corrects you. For the LORD disciplines those he loves, and he punishes each one he accepts as his child." (Hebrews chapter 12 verses 5 and 6 - NLT)

If God is so wonderful, why didn't he create a world without suffering?

The simple answer to that question is: **God did**.

'God saw all that he had made, and it was very good.'
(Genesis chapter 1 verse 31 NIV)

Things only began to go wrong when sin entered the world after the serpent, Satan, succeeded in deceiving Eve in the Garden of Eden.

As a result of sin entering the world, bad things happen. God created a world that was good, but sin has messed everything up.

Jesus said that, *"Here on earth you will have many trials and sorrows. But take heart, because I have overcome the world"* (John chapter 16 verse 33 - NLT) God knows that we will all suffer troubles, but he gives us great hope because Jesus Christ defeated death when he was resurrected from the grave.

Being a Christian doesn't make you immune to trouble.
Bad things can happen to good people.
And good things can happen to bad people.

It would be wrong for us to expect God to solve all of our problems. This would be diluting God to the level of a car breakdown service.

It would be shamefully shallow of us to expect God to

act like a one-stop fix-it shop for all our troubles. Why should we expect God to allow us to reduce his dealings with us to formula that *we* think should work?

But it doesn't mean that God has forgotten about us and about our troubles in this world.

God loves the world so much that he has provided us with the solution to sin.

God loves the world so much that he gave us hope.

"For God so loved the world, that he gave his only Son, that whoever believes in him should not perish but have eternal life. For God did not send his Son into the world to condemn the world, but in order that the world might be saved through him."   (John chapter 3 verses 16 and 17 - ESV)

Jesus Christ is the solution to this world of suffering that has been caused by sin.

The death of Jesus Christ was the sacrifice that God required to forgive the sins of the world.

And on the third day after he was killed, Jesus was resurrected from the dead.

Jesus Christ defeated death.

Paul explains what this means to you and me, when he asks, *'have you forgotten that when we were joined with Christ Jesus in baptism, we joined him in his death? For we died and were buried with Christ by baptism. And just as Christ was raised from the dead by the glorious power of the Father, now we also may live new lives. Since we have been united with him in his death, we will also be raised to life as he was. We know that our old sinful selves were crucified with Christ so that sin might lose its power in our lives. We*

are no longer slaves to sin. For when we died with Christ we were set free from the power of sin. And since we died with Christ, we know we will also live with him. We are sure of this because Christ was raised from the dead, and he will never die again. Death no longer has any power over him. When he died, he died once to break the power of sin. But now that he lives, he lives for the glory of God. So you also should consider yourselves to be dead to the power of sin and alive to God through Christ Jesus.'
(Romans chapter 6 verses 3 to 11 - NLT)

What has God done to save us from suffering?

God gave his only Son.

Suffering is the effect that is caused by sin.

Logically: if you remove the cause, you solve the effect.

In other words: if sin is removed, suffering ends.

Let me illustrate this for you: -

Imagine a nice sharp pencil.

Now, imagine this nice sharp pencil pressing against your naked eyeball.

The pain in your eye is the *effect* of having the pencil stuck in it: the pencil has *caused* the pain.

If you apply anesthetic pain-relief to your eyeball, it will help to reduce the agony, but it does not remove the pencil. To cure your painful eye problem, you need to completely remove the pencil.

Asking God to remove your suffering is like asking him to apply some anesthetic ointment to your problem.

What you really need God to do is to remove the cause of the problem.

The good news is that God has already provided the solution that saves us from the cause of the problem, and it's up to each of us to decide whether we accept this salvation, or not.

The solution to the cause of our troubles is clearly identified when Jesus Christ states: *"This is how much God loved the world: He gave his Son, his one and only Son. And this is why: so that no one need be destroyed; by believing in him, anyone can have a whole and lasting life. God didn't go to all the trouble of sending his Son merely to point an accusing finger, telling the world how bad it was. He came to help, to put the world right again. Anyone who trusts in him is acquitted; anyone who refuses to trust him has long since been under the death sentence without knowing it. And why? Because of that person's failure to believe in the one-of-a-kind Son of God when introduced to him."* (John chapter 3 verses 16 and 17 - MSG)

In this world we suffer a multitude of troubles: murder, injustice, sex crimes, bullies, jealousy, war, genocide, intolerance, and hatred,... (*just to name a few*).

The troubles in this world are the effects of sin.
John touches on this when he warns: *'We know that we are children of God and that the world around us is under the control of the evil one.'* (1 John chapter 5 verse 19 - NLT)
If you ask why God doesn't step in and solve the *effects* of sin, you are failing to realize is that God has already offered the solution to the *cause* of these problems: through the sacrifice of Jesus Christ, God has provided the solution to sin, and defeated death.

Paul declared the good news that Jesus Christ, *'has appeared once for all at the culmination of the ages to do away with sin by the sacrifice of himself. Just as people are destined to die once, and after that to face judgment, so Christ was sacrificed once to take away the sins of many; and he will appear a second time, not to bear sin, but to bring salvation to those who are waiting for him.'*
(Hebrews chapter 9 verses 26 to 28 - NIV)

If God exists, why do so many people suffer hunger and poverty?

The world has plenty of food to feed everyone, but it is the irresponsibility and greed of everyone else that prevents this food from being shared evenly with those in need.

'Do not love this world nor the things it offers you, for when you love the world, you do not have the love of the Father in you. For the world offers only a craving for physical pleasure, a craving for everything we see, and pride in our achievements and possessions. These are not from the Father, but are from this world.'
(1 John chapter 2 verses 15 and 16 - NLT)

Why does God allow natural disasters?

If you are expecting me to convince you that God has never had anything to do with natural disasters: I can't.

God is responsible for perhaps the single greatest natural disaster ever recorded in human history.

In Genesis, God told Noah that, *'I'm going to bring a flood on the Earth that will destroy everything alive under Heaven. Total destruction.'* (Genesis chapter 6 verse 17 - MSG)

God only allowed Noah and his family to survive with the ark full of animals.

For the Passover, God sent death to the firstborn of an entire nation: *'And that night at midnight, the LORD struck down all the firstborn sons in the land of Egypt, from the firstborn son of Pharaoh, who sat on his throne, to the firstborn son of the prisoner in the dungeon. Even the firstborn of their livestock were killed. Pharaoh and all his officials and all the people of Egypt woke up during the night, and loud wailing was heard throughout the land of Egypt. There was not a single house where someone had not died.'* (Exodus chapter 12 verses 29 and 30 - NLT)

'And don't forget Sodom and Gomorrah and their neighboring towns, which were filled with immorality and every kind of sexual perversion. Those cities were destroyed by fire and serve as a warning of the eternal fire of God's judgment.' (Jude verse 7 - NLT)

God told Moses what would happen when his people begin to worship foreign gods and abandon the one true God. God warned Moses: *"Then my anger will blaze forth against them. I will abandon them, hiding my face from them, and they will be devoured. Terrible trouble will come down on them, and on that day they will say, 'These disasters have come down on us because God is no longer among us!' At that time I will hide my face from them on account of all the evil they commit by worshiping other gods."* (Deuteronomy chapter 31 verses 17 and 18 - NLT)

In the **Old Testament** relationship, God is responsible for sending disasters on wicked people.

Now, in the **New Testament** relationship, God applies the new solution to sin: -

God does not send disasters to kill sinners: God responds to our sin with the opportunity of forgiveness. God gave his Son to save sinners.

The disasters that affect the world today are not caused by God. The disasters that affect the world today are caused by the fact that we live in an imperfect world where bad things happen. And Satan is active in the world, so we can expect all sorts of troubles.

'We are not fighting against flesh-and-blood enemies, but against evil rulers and authorities of the unseen world, against mighty powers in this dark world, and against evil spirits in the heavenly places.'
(Ephesians chapter 6 verse 12 - NLT)

In the book of Job chapter 1, Satan ridicules God's most obedient and trusting believer: a man called Job.

Satan ridiculed Job, reasoning that the only reason why Job was obedient and true to God was because God had been so generous to Job.

God permitted Satan to test the faithfulness of Job: *"All right, you may test him," the* LORD *said to Satan. "Do whatever you want with everything he possesses, but don't harm him physically." So Satan left the* LORD*'s presence.'*
(Job chapter 1 verse 12 - NLT)

Satan brought down disaster after disaster on poor Job. His oxen and donkeys were stolen and the farm workers were killed in the fields. Fire fell from the sky and burnt up his sheep and his shepherds. Raiders stole his camels and killed his servants. A powerful wind blew down the house where his sons and daughters were feasting, and all were killed.

Satan also brought disease to Job, *'and he struck Job with terrible boils from head to foot.'*
(Job chapter 2 verse 7 - NLT)

Satan caused fire to fall from the sky. Satan caused the wind to tear down the house, killing Job's children. Satan caused the disease that afflicted Job with terrible boils.

God did not cause these things to happen to Job: Satan was the cause. And Satan continues to be the cause of many terrible disasters that we suffer today.

What's going to happen to Satan?

The end awaiting Satan is revealed to John in the book of Revelation: *"Then the devil, who had deceived them, was thrown into the fiery lake of burning sulfur, joining the beast and the false prophet. There they will be tormented day and night forever and ever."*
(Revelation chapter 20 verse 10 - NLT)

The future for people who are saved is also revealed to John in the book of Revelation, and it is wonderful: *'And I heard a great voice out of heaven saying, "Behold, the tabernacle of God is with men, and he will dwell with them, and they shall be his people, and God himself shall be with them, and be their God." And God shall wipe away all tears from their eyes; and there shall be no more death, neither sorrow, nor crying, neither shall there be any more pain: for the former things are passed away.'*
(Revelation chapter 21 verses 3 and 4 - KJV)

Still not convinced that God exists?

If you are still struggling to believe in God, there may be a very good reason: *'Satan, who is the god of this world, has blinded the minds of those who don't believe. They are unable to see the glorious light of the Good News. They don't understand this message about the glory of Christ, who is the exact likeness of God.'*
(2 Corinthians chapter 4 verse 4 - NLT)

Do not let the devil blind your mind to God.

Open your mind, and open your heart to the good message and true hope that Jesus Christ suffered so much to bring to you.

If you still do not believe in God: Realize the truth that God believes in you.

Who is God?

God is the holy, holy, holy, almighty, all-knowing and everlasting God. And to a believer, God is your loving and ever-faithful Father.

God's Chosen People

God told Abram that his descendants would become a great nation. God told Abram: *"and in you all the families of the earth shall be blessed."*
(Genesis chapter 12 verse 3 - ESV)

In Deuteronomy chapter 7, these descendents of Abram who have escaped from slavery in Egypt, are told that they are the people who are holy to God, and that God has chosen them to be his treasured possession.

These people are the Jews, and they remain God's chosen people, and they enjoy a special relationship with God throughout the Old Testament. When they are good and obedient, God rewards them; and when they neglect God and disobey his instructions, he punishes them. This is fatherly love.

The New Testament delivers a new promise from God. The New Testament delivers a new relationship with God.

"God so loved the world, that he gave his only Son, that whosoever believes in him should not perish but have eternal life." (John chapter 3 verse 16 - ESV)

God sent his Son, Jesus Christ, as a gift available to everyone, (not just Jews), but to **everyone** who believes in him.

It is important to remember that God told Abram that, *"in you all the families of the earth shall be blessed,"* because Jesus, through his adopting Father Joseph, was a direct descendent of Abram, which means that Jesus is the fulfillment of God's promise to Abram.

Through Abram all Jews are identified as God's chosen people. (God changed Abram's name to Abraham at Genesis chapter 17 verse 5.)

Through the sacrifice that Jesus Christ suffered on the cross, everyone who believes becomes one of God's chosen people.

"In Christ's family there can be no division into Jew and non-Jew, slave and free, male and female. Among us you are all equal. That is, we are all in a common relationship with Jesus Christ. Also, since you are Christ's family, then you are Abraham's famous "descendant," heirs according to the covenant promises."
(Galatians chapter 3 verses 28 and 29 - MSG)

Jesus Christ was the sacrifice that God needed to forgive our sins - *your sins and my sins.*

Jesus Christ accepted the punishment for our sins, and was sacrificed to accept the punishment for all the wrong things that we have done and said and thought.

Through this amazing act of love, you can become one of God's chosen people: you can become a child of God.

Through Jesus Christ everyone is welcome

Peter explains this, stating that Christians, *'are a chosen people, a royal priesthood, a holy nation, God's special possession, that you may declare the praises of him who called you out of darkness into his wonderful light. Once you were not a people, but now you are the people of God; once you had not received mercy, but now you have received mercy."* (1 Peter chapter 2 verses 9 and 10 - NIV)

God's chosen people of the Old Testament had exclusively been the Jews.

But with the New Testament, after the sacrifice that Jesus Christ made on the cross, anyone can become one of God's chosen people, when they believe.

When you ask God to forgive your sins, when you ask God to forgive you for all the wrong things you have ever done or thought or said, God does not get angry and punish you. Instead, God accepts you as one of his children, because Jesus Christ has already accepted your punishment; Jesus Christ has already made the sacrifice that was needed to compensate God for your sins when he accepted that terrible death on a cross.

'For it is by grace you have been saved, through faith - and this is not from yourselves, it is the gift of God - not by works, so that none may boast.'
(Ephesians chapter 2 verses 8 and 9 - NIV)

Gospel

The word *Gospel* comes from the combination of two Old English words: *god* meaning **good**, and *spell* meaning **message**: *godspell*.

The Gospel literally means the Good Message.

So, the Gospel of Matthew can be read as the *Good Message of Matthew*; Matthew has written his account of the life of Jesus, which is a good message because it is the fulfillment of God's promise through Jesus Christ, whose sacrifice has brought the opportunity of salvation to you and me. And that's a *very* good message.

There are four books in the New Testament called the Gospels. These are the good messages written by **Matthew**, **Mark**, **Luke**, and **John**, which are the first four books of the New Testament.

In the Gospel of Mark, Jesus instructed his disciples to, *"Go into all the world and preach the gospel to all creation. Whoever believes and is baptized will be saved, but whoever does not believe will be condemned."*
(Mark chapter 16 verses 15 and 16 - NIV)

Grace

The word *grace* comes from the Greek word *chairo*, which is a word that is used to indicate favor, goodwill, and loving kindness, particularly when this favor, goodwill and loving kindness is granted by a powerful person to a weak person.

To illustrate this, imagine a wealthy landowner who must decide what to do with a poor man who has been caught stealing his prize duck. The gamekeeper has caught the poor man in the act, and dragged him and the dead duck up to the big house to face the landowner. The wealthy landowner has the legal right and every good reason to call the Police, have the man arrested, and see him justly punished for his crime.

But instead of punishing the poor man, the wealthy landowner forgives him.

This is grace.

There is another [non-Christian] concept of receiving favor or forgiveness, which is called karma.

Karma is the complete opposite of Grace.

Karma is all about getting what you deserve: karma is the assumed result of a random act of kindness on a stranger, whereupon you will benefit from your kindness by receiving good things in return; likewise, if you do something harmful to another person, you can expect something harmful to happen to you.

Grace is the opposite of karma. Grace is exclusively about receiving what you do not deserve.

None of us deserves forgiveness of our sins, but God gave his only Son as the sacrifice that has allowed God to forgive our sins.

Paul explained that, *'everyone has sinned; we all fall short of God's glorious standard. Yet God, in his grace, freely makes us right in his sight. He did this through Christ Jesus when he freed us from the penalty for our sins.'*
(Romans chapter 3 verses 23 and 24 - NLT)

You cannot earn forgiveness from God.

You cannot buy forgiveness from God.

Forgiveness is a gift from God, which we definitely do not deserve.

If you think that you can win God's grace by giving all your property to charity and spending all your time caring for people in need - you are wrong.

Paul explains it plainly when he states that God's favor, *'cannot be based on works; if it were, grace would no longer be grace.'* (Romans chapter 11 verse 6 - NIV)

We cannot earn God's grace.

God's gift of salvation is given freely.

If we could earn God's forgiveness by doing good works, it would mean that the sacrifice that Jesus Christ made on the cross was meaningless.

Why would God send his only Son to die on a cross if we could simply earn salvation?

'For it is by grace you have been saved, through faith—and this is not from yourselves, it is the gift of God—not by works, so that no one can boast.'
(Ephesians chapter 2 verses 8 and 9 - NIV)

As a Christian, you need to be graceful.

Paul instructs us to, *'Be kind and compassionate to one another, forgiving each other, just as in Christ, God forgave you.'* (Ephesians chapter 4 verse 32 - NIV)

As Christians, we have received grace; and as Christians we should live a life of grace.

It is easy to be kind and forgiving to other Christians, but Jesus tells us that we should love our enemies.

"If you love those who love you, what credit is that to you? Even sinners love those who love them. And if you do good to those who are good to you, what credit is that to you? Even sinners do that. And if you lend to those from whom you expect repayment, what credit is that to you? Even sinners lend to sinners, expecting to be repaid in full. But love your enemies, do good to them, and lend to them without expecting to get anything back. Then your reward will be great, and you will be children of the Most High, because he is kind to the ungrateful and wicked. Be merciful, just as your Father is merciful."
(Luke chapter 6 verses 32 to 36 - NIV)

Here, Jesus is telling us to be like him, to give without expecting anything in return, just as we have been given God's forgiveness and unconditional love.

This is grace.

Heaven

When you think of heaven, perhaps you imagine an airy-fairy place filled with little fluffy clouds and beautiful happy people floating about on big white wings.

That sounds nice, but the real heaven is really, truly amazing.

In the English translations of the Bible, the word heaven is used to describe three different environments: -

1. Heaven is the sky, where the birds fly about.

2. Heaven is the outer space of planets and stars.

3. Heaven is God's home.

If you want to know more about the first two heavens, you're reading the wrong book. I will try to describe the third heaven, the heaven that is God's home.

Heaven is revealed to us through eyewitness accounts in the Bible.

In Paul's second letter to the Christians in Corinth, he explains how he was elevated into heaven where had his enlightening, life-changing experience with Jesus Christ: *'I was caught up to the third heaven fourteen years ago. Whether I was in my body or out of my body, I don't know—only God knows. Yes, only God knows whether I was in my body or outside my body. But I do know that I was caught up to paradise and heard things so astounding that they cannot be expressed in words, things no human is allowed to tell.'*

(2 Corinthians chapter 12 verses 2 to 4 - NLT)

In the scene described in the book of Acts chapter 7, the people have concocted lies about the disciple Stephen to condemn him, and he has been dragged before the Council and the Chief Priest to defend himself against these false accusations. After Stephen has explained the truth about Jesus Christ, he accused the Council of disobeying God's law. *'The Jewish leaders were infuriated by Stephen's accusation, and they shook their fists at him in rage. But Stephen, full of the Holy Spirit, gazed steadily into heaven and saw the glory of God, and he saw Jesus standing in the place of honor at God's right hand. And he told them, "Look, I see the heavens opened and the Son of Man standing in the place of honor at God's right hand!"* (Acts chapter 7 verses 54 to 56 - NLT)

Heaven is absolutely amazing.

Where is heaven?

Heaven is the sky above us; heaven is the universe where all the planets and stars have been placed; and heaven is the place where God resides.

I can point at the sky. I can point to the moon and the stars. But the Bible does not identify a physical location for heaven.

'So then the Lord Jesus, after he had spoken to them, was taken up into heaven and sat down at the right hand of God.' (Mark chapter 16 verse 19 - ESV)

"In my Father's house are many mansions: if it were not so, I would have told you. I go to prepare a place for you." (John chapter 14 verse 2 - KJV)

Heaven is a real place, it is a spiritual place where Jesus Christ is preparing accommodation for his believers.

What does heaven look like?

In the book of Revelation, John gave this amazing description of heaven: *"I saw a door standing open in heaven, and the same voice I had heard before spoke to me like a trumpet blast. The voice said, "Come up here, and I will show you what must happen after this."*

And instantly I was in the Spirit, and I saw a throne in heaven and someone sitting on it. The one sitting on the throne was as brilliant as gemstones—like jasper and carnelian. And the glow of an emerald circled his throne like a rainbow. Twenty-four thrones surrounded him, and twenty-four elders sat on them. They were all clothed in white and had gold crowns on their heads. From the throne came flashes of lightning and the rumble of thunder. And in front of the throne were seven torches with burning flames. This is the sevenfold Spirit of God. In front of the throne was a shiny sea of glass, sparkling like crystal. In the centre and around the throne were four living beings, each covered with eyes, front and back. The first of these living beings was like a lion; the second was like an ox; the third had a human face; and the fourth was like an eagle in flight. Each of these living beings had six wings, and their wings were covered all over with eyes, inside and out. Day after day and night after night they keep on saying, "Holy, holy, holy is the LORD God, the Almighty—the one who always was, who is, and who is still to come." Whenever the living beings give glory and honor and thanks to the one sitting on the throne (the one who lives forever and ever), the twenty-four elders fall down and worship the one sitting on the throne (the one who lives forever and ever). And they lay

their crowns before the throne and say, "You are worthy, O LORD our God, to receive glory and honor and power. For you created all things, and they exist because you created what you pleased."
(Revelation chapter 4 - NLT)

How can you get to heaven?

Being good will not get you into heaven.

Being nice will not get you into heaven.

Memorizing the entire Bible will not get you into heaven.

Going to church every Sunday will not get you into heaven.

Giving all your property and money away to charity, and spending the rest of your life helping people in need, will not get you into heaven.

There is only one way to reach heaven: **Believe**

Being nice and good, and attending church, and learning from the Bible, and being generous to others: these are all virtuous qualities, but you can't buy or bribe or earn your way into God's favor.

However, *"if you confess with your mouth that Jesus is Lord and believe in your heart that God raised him from the dead, you will be saved. For with the heart one believes and is justified, and with the mouth one confesses and is saved."*
(Romans chapter 10 verses 9 and 10 - ESV)

You and me: we are sinners.

We do not deserve God's love.

We do not deserve God's forgiveness.

We do not deserve a reserved place in heaven.

However, God loves you.

God loves you, despite all the shameful sins that you are guilty of. And because God loves you, God has made an amazing sacrifice that has compensated for all of your sins.

That amazing sacrifice was the death of his only Son, Jesus Christ.

When you realize that Jesus Christ has already made the sacrifice that has allowed God to forgive your sins, and when you ask God for forgiveness, a place is reserved for you in heaven.

You do not need to memorize the Bible to be saved.
You do not need to pass any exams or interviews.
You just need to believe, and ask God for forgiveness.

I was just a boy when I asked God for forgiveness, and my prayer was just six simple words: "God I'm ashamed; please forgive me." God blessed me with the gift of his Holy Spirit: I knew that he had forgiven me, and my life was changed forever.

Believe with all your heart, and you will be saved.

"This is how much God loved the world: He gave his Son, his one and only Son. And this is why: so that no one need be destroyed; by believing in him, anyone can have a whole and lasting life. God didn't go to all the trouble of sending his Son merely to point an accusing finger, telling the world how bad it was. He came to help, to put the world right again." (John chapter 3 verses 16 and 17 - MSG)

When you believe in the sacrifice that Jesus Christ

made on your behalf, you will secure a reserved place in heaven.

Jesus told his disciples: *"Don't let your hearts be troubled. Trust in God, and trust also in me. There is more than enough room in my Father's home. If this were not so, would I have told you that I am going to prepare a place for you? When everything is ready, I will come and get you, so that you will always be with me where I am."*
(John chapter 14 verses 1 to 3 - NLT)

What is the alternative place to heaven?

Oh!

It's not a good place.

It is definitely not an attractive option.

The alternative destination for your soul is described in the book of Revelation: *"But as for the cowardly, the faithless, the detestable, as for murderers, the sexually immoral, sorcerers, idolaters, and all liars, their portion will be in the lake that burns with fire and sulfur, which is the second death."* (Revelation chapter 21 verse 8 - ESV)

There is no final middle place.

The only alternative to heaven is the lake of fire.

What will heaven be like?

'No eye has seen, no ear has heard, and no mind has imagined what God has prepared for those who love him.'
(1 Corinthians chapter 2 verse 9 - NLT)

I know that when I die, my soul is going to heaven.

I know this is true, because this is the good message of the New Testament.

When you believe that Jesus Christ suffered and died on the cross to pay the price of punishment for your sins, you can be assured that when you die your soul will also enjoy a place in heaven.

Hell

Perhaps you imagine hell to be something resembling a deep, dark, dismal cavern illuminated by a pool of bubbling lava. According to the Bible, the place for the unsaved will be something like that.

Something like that,

But not yet,....

When hell is mentioned throughout the English translations of the Bible, it isn't always referring to the same place or condition of suffering for human souls.

If fact, the word *hell* isn't even a biblical word.

Hell is an old pagan European word for a covered or hidden place; but the word *hell* has been adopted by many of the English translators of the Bible.

Throughout the Old Testament, references to hell are made in the original Hebrew language of the Bible using the word *Sheol*.

Some Bible translations don't use the word *hell* in their Old Testament translations: *the underworld* (NLT); *the realm of the dead* (NIV); *Sheol* (ESV).

In the Old Testament, when an ungodly person died, their soul separated from their body: their dead body was put into a grave, and their soul went to this place called Sheol.

Sheol is the place of the dead.

Sheol is a hopeless place of emptiness.

Sheol is a place of complete separation from God.

In the world-weary book of Ecclesiastes, the preacher

says: *'Whatever your hand finds to do, do it with your might, for there is no work or thought or knowledge or wisdom in Sheol, to which you are going.'*
(Ecclesiastes chapter 9 verse 10 - ESV)

The souls of all people who have died without asking God to forgive their sins, go to Sheol.

In the book of Psalms, David praises God saying: *'Therefore my heart is glad, and my whole being rejoices; my flesh also dwells secure. For you will not abandon my soul to Sheol, or let your holy one see corruption.'*
(Psalm 16 verses 9 and 10 - ESV)

The **New Testament** references to hell are different.

Hell is referred to in two separate contexts: -

CONTEXT 1: Hell is written in the original language of the Bible as *Hades*.

Hades is the same place as Sheol.

The reason for using a different word for the same place is because the Old Testament was written in Hebrew, and the New Testament was written in Greek. *Hades* is the Greek word for *Sheol* - it is the same word in a different language.

As with Sheol in the Old Testament, Hades is the place where your soul goes when your body dies. Hades is a hopeless place of emptiness where the souls of unbelievers are completely separated from God.

CONTEXT 2: Hell is written in the original language of the New Testament as, *Gehenna*.

Gehenna probably resembles the popular image of hell. Gehenna was a hopeless place of perpetual fire and suffering.

Quite literally, Gehenna was the place where all the rubbish and waste from the city of Jerusalem was taken to be dumped and burnt.

Gehenna was situated outside the city walls of Jerusalem, in the Valley of Hinnom; it is where some of the kings of Judah had sacrificed their children by fire, which is described in the book of Jeremiah, when God complains that the people of Judah, *'have built pagan shrines at Topheth, the garbage dump in the valley of Ben-Hinnom, and there they burn their sons and daughters in the fire.'* (Jeremiah chapter 7 verse 31 - NLT)

God complained that: *"Israel has forsaken me and turned this valley into a place of wickedness. The people burn incense to foreign gods—idols never before acknowledged by this generation, by their ancestors, or by the kings of Judah. And they have filled this place with the blood of innocent children. They have built pagan shrines to Baal, and there they burn their sons as sacrifices to Baal. I have never commanded such a horrible deed; it never even crossed my mind to command such a thing! So beware, for the time is coming, says the LORD, when this garbage dump will no longer be called Topheth or the valley of Ben-Hinnom, but the Valley of Slaughter.'*
(Jeremiah chapter 19 verses 4 to 6 - NLT)

Here, in the book of Jeremiah, God has cursed this place called Gehenna in the Hinnon Valley; and centuries later in the time of Jesus, it is being used as the appropriate location for the city dump.

Jesus Christ used Gehenna as a metaphor for what will happen to the souls of those who mislead people from

God's truth; Jesus scolds them, saying, *"Snakes! Sons of vipers! How will you escape the judgment of hell?* [Gehenna]*"* (Matthew chapter 23 verse 33 - NLT)

Again in the Gospel of Mark, Jesus explained to his disciples about the dangers of being led into sin: *"So if your hand makes you lose your faith, cut it off! It is better for you to enter life without a hand than to keep both hands and go off to hell* [Gehenna], *to the fire that never goes out. And if your foot makes you lose your faith, cut it off! It is better for you to enter life without a foot than to keep both feet and be thrown into hell* [Gehenna]. *And if your eye makes you lose your faith, take it out! It is better for you to enter the Kingdom of God with only one eye than to keep both eyes and be thrown into hell* [Gehenna]*"*
(Mark chapter 9 verses 43 to 47 - NLT)

In each of these references to hell, Jesus uses the word *Gehenna*, which is the name of the Jerusalem city dump where all the rubbish was tossed and burnt.

"There 'the worms that eat them never die, and the fire that burns them is never put out.'" (Mark chapter 9 verse 48 - NLT)
What Jesus said here in verse 48, is a direct quotation from the book of Isaiah, when God told Isaiah what the future will be like when God judges the world: *"And they will go out and look on the dead bodies of those who rebelled against me; the worms that eat them will not die, the fire that burns them will not be quenched, and they will be loathsome to all mankind."* (Isaiah chapter 66 verse 24 - NIV)

So, there appear to be two places for the souls of people who do not believe in God: -

1. Sheol/Hades, which is a hopeless place of emptiness and complete separation from God.

2. The fire, which Jesus likened to the unending fires of the Jerusalem city dump.

When Jesus used the comparison of the city dump for the place where unrighteous souls are thrown, you can really appreciate what a horrible fate this is for your soul.

Not only will your soul be completely separated from God and cast into the dump with all the other rubbish, but your soul will also suffer the agony of burning in a fire that never goes out.

Which place do the souls of unsaved people go to?

To the place of emptiness and hopelessness and complete separation from God?

Or, the place that resembles the hopelessness, suffering and perpetual fires of the Jerusalem city dump?

Unfortunately: both places.

This truth is clarified in the last book of the Bible, when John describes what Jesus Christ reveals to him.

'I saw a Great White Throne and the One Enthroned. Nothing could stand before or against the Presence, nothing in Heaven, nothing on earth. And then I saw all the dead, great and small, standing there—before the Throne! And books were opened. Then another book was opened: the Book of Life. The dead were judged by what was written in the books, by the way they had lived. Sea released its dead, Death and Hell turned in their dead. Each man and woman was judged by the way he or she had lived. Then Death and

Hell were hurled into Lake Fire. This is the second death—Lake Fire. Anyone whose name was not found inscribed in the Book of Life was hurled into Lake Fire."
(Revelation chapter 20 verses 11 to 15 - MSG)

This revelation should make you sit up and pay attention. Because if you die in your sinful condition your soul will go to the hopeless place of emptiness and complete separation from God. And ultimately, there will be a Judgment.

At the Judgment, all the souls that have been waiting in the hopeless place of emptiness and complete separation from God, whose names are not written in the Book of Life, will be thrown into the Lake of Fire.

Jesus explained to his disciples what will happen at the end of the world: *"The Son of Man will send his angels, and they will remove from his Kingdom everything that causes sin and all who do evil. And the angels will throw them into the fiery furnace, where there will be weeping and gnashing of teeth. Then the righteous will shine like the sun in their Father's Kingdom."*
(Matthew chapter 13 verses 41 to 43 - NLT)

And a few verses later, Jesus repeats his warning, stating: *"The angels will come and separate the wicked people from the righteous, throwing the wicked into the fiery furnace, where there will be weeping and gnashing of teeth."* (Matthew chapter 13 verses 49 and 50 - NLT)

In both of these statements, Jesus does not use the word Sheol, or Hades, or Gehenna: Jesus states very clearly that the souls of people who are not righteous will be ***thrown into the fire***.

"But as for the cowardly, the faithless, the detestable, as for murderers, the sexually immoral, sorcerers, idolaters, and all liars, their portion will be in the lake that burns with fire and sulfur, which is the second death."
(Revelation chapter 21 verse 8 - ESV)

Don't be thinking that the Lake of Fire will be the end of the matter, that your soul will finally be burnt up, and your suffering finally extinguished to nothingness.

I'm afraid that's not the end of your misery.

'Then the devil, who had deceived them, was thrown into the fiery lake of burning sulfur, joining the beast and the false prophet. There they will be tormented day and night forever and ever." (Revelation chapter 20 verse 10 - NLT)

Forever and ever, that's an eternity of suffering.

Why risk eternal suffering, when God freely offers you salvation?

"For God so loved the world, that he gave his only Son, that whoever believes in him should not perish but have eternal life. For God did not send his Son into the world to condemn the world, but in order that the world might be saved through him"
(John chapter 3 verses 16 and 17 - ESV)

I know that when I die, my soul will not end up in the Lake of Fire. I know this because when I asked God to forgive my sins, he forgave me: I have been saved from that destiny: this is the good message that the New Testament makes this perfectly clear many times over.

"The message is very close at hand; it is on your lips and in your heart." And that message is the very message about

faith that we preach: If you openly declare that Jesus is Lord and believe in your heart that God raised him from the dead, you will be saved. For it is by believing in your heart that you are made right with God, and it is by openly declaring your faith that you are saved.'

(Romans chapter 10 verses 8 to 10 - NLT)

Holy

Christian believers are instructed to be holy.
To be holy means to be distinct, to be separate, to be different in a special way.

Paul says that we should, *'Work at living in peace with everyone, and work at living a holy life, for those who are not holy will not see the Lord.'*
(Hebrews chapter 12 verse 14 - NLT)

It is important to be holy, because those who are not holy will not see God.
'I urge you, brothers and sisters, in view of God's mercy, to offer your bodies as a living sacrifice, holy and pleasing to God—this is your true and proper worship.'
(Romans chapter 12 verse 1 - NIV)

What does it mean to be holy?
'Live as God's obedient children. Don't slip back into your old ways of living to satisfy your own desires. You didn't know any better then. But now you must be holy in everything you do, just as God who chose you is holy. For the Scriptures say, "You must be holy because I am holy."
(1 Peter chapter 1 verses 14 to 16 - NLT)

Being a Christian isn't just about being holy on Sundays. Being a Christian means embracing a change in attitude to your lifestyle and behavior in every aspect of what you do and say and think, and maintaining this change throughout your everyday life.

'Take your everyday, ordinary life—your sleeping, eating, going-to-work, and walking-around life—and place it

before God as an offering. Embracing what God does for you is the best thing you can do for him. Don't become so well-adjusted to your culture that you fit into it without even thinking. Instead, fix your attention on God. You'll be changed from the inside out. Readily recognize what he wants from you, and quickly respond to it. Unlike the culture around you, always dragging you down to its level of immaturity, God brings the best out of you, develops well-formed maturity in you.'
(Romans chapter 12 verses 1 and 2 - MSG)

Paul illustrates how we should separate ourselves from the ordinary to become holy, using the example of kitchen utensils: *'In a well-furnished kitchen there are not only crystal goblets and silver platters, but waste cans and compost buckets—some containers used to serve fine meals, others to take out the garbage. Become the kind of container God can use to present any and every kind of gift to his guests for their blessing.*

Run away from infantile indulgence. Run after mature righteousness—faith, love, peace—joining those who are in honest and serious prayer before God. Refuse to get involved in inane discussions; they always end up in fights. God's servant must not be argumentative, but a gentle listener and a teacher who keeps cool, working firmly but patiently with those who refuse to obey.
(2 Timothy chapter 2 verses 20 to 25 - MSG)

As a Christian, how can I be holy?
When you ask God to forgive your sins, God gives you a gift: you receive his Holy Spirit.

The Holy Spirit lives within you.

'The Holy Spirit produces this kind of fruit in our lives: love, joy, peace, patience, kindness, goodness, faithfulness, gentleness, and self-control. There is no law against these things!

Those who belong to Christ Jesus have nailed the passions and desires of their sinful nature to his cross and crucified them there. Since we are living by the Spirit, let us follow the Spirit's leading in every part of our lives. Let us not become conceited, or provoke one another, or be jealous of one another.'

(Galatians chapter 5 verses 22 to 26 - NLT)

The Holy Spirit provides you with the strength and confidence that you need to change your life.

'At one time we too were foolish, disobedient, deceived and enslaved by all kinds of passions and pleasures. We lived in malice and envy, being hated and hating one another. But when the kindness and love of God our Savior appeared, he saved us, not because of righteous things we had done, but because of his mercy. He saved us through the washing of rebirth and renewal by the Holy Spirit, whom he poured out on us generously through Jesus Christ our Savior, so that, having been justified by his grace, we might become heirs having the hope of eternal life.'

(Titus chapter 3 verses 3 to 7 - NIV)

When you believe in God and ask him to forgive your sins, you are effectively reborn into a new life where you have become dead to sin, and alive to God.

This gift of the Holy Spirit that God gives you when you believe, helps you to leave your old sinful life behind.

The Holy Spirit helps you to lead a holy life.

'If we get included in Christ's sin-conquering death, we also get included in his life-saving resurrection. We know that when Jesus was raised from the dead it was a signal of the end of death-as-the-end. Never again will death have the last word. When Jesus died, he took sin down with him, but alive he brings God down to us. From now on, think of it this way: Sin speaks a dead language that means nothing to you; God speaks your mother tongue, and you hang on every word. You are dead to sin and alive to God. That's what Jesus did.

That means you must not give sin a vote in the way you conduct your lives. Don't give it the time of day. Don't even run little errands that are connected with that old way of life. Throw yourselves wholeheartedly and full-time— remember, you've been raised from the dead!—into God's way of doing things. Sin can't tell you how to live. After all, you're not living under that old tyranny any longer. You're living in the freedom of God.'

(Romans chapter 6 verse 8 to 14 - MSG)

Leading a holy life

'Work hard to show the results of your salvation, obeying God with deep reverence and fear. For God is working in you, giving you the desire and the power to do what pleases him.' (Philippians chapter 2 verses 12 and 13 - NLT)

With God working within you, you have the ability to lead a holy life.

Pursuing a holy life requires us to focus ourselves on what is pleasing to God in everything that we do, in everything that we say, and in everything that we think.

By not leading a holy life, you are rejecting God.

'God's will is for you to be holy, so stay away from all sexual sin. Then each of you will control his own body and live in holiness and honor—not in lustful passion like the pagans who do not know God and his ways. Never harm or cheat a fellow believer in this matter by violating his wife, for the Lord avenges all such sins, as we have solemnly warned you before. God has called us to live holy lives, not impure lives. Therefore, anyone who refuses to live by these rules is not disobeying human teaching but is rejecting God, who gives his Holy Spirit to you.'

(1 Thessalonians chapter 4 verses 3 to 8 - NLT)

Being holy is to separate yourself from the ways of the world. Being holy does not mean that you should separate yourself *from* the world; you should separate yourself from the *ways* of the world.

Following the fashionable opinions and ways of the world is often the easiest thing to do; this herd instinct of following the crowd comes naturally to most of us.

Separating yourself from the world and leading a holy life can be difficult for many people, and Jesus Christ knows this. Jesus Christ warned his disciples that, *"You can enter God's Kingdom only through the narrow gate. The highway to hell is broad, and its gate is wide for the many who choose that way. But the gateway to life is very narrow and the road is difficult, and only a few ever find it."*

(Matthew chapter 7 verses 13 and 14 - NLT)

Being holy is to leave behind the lusts and desires of a worldly life.

Being holy is to lead a life that is Christ-like.

God is *holy, holy, holy*

In the vision of heaven that is described by Isaiah, the seraphim angels continuously fly around the throne of God calling, *"Holy, holy, holy is the Lord of hosts; the whole earth is full of his glory."*
(Isaiah chapter 6 verse 3 - ESV)

And in the last book of the Bible, John describes the heavenly creatures around the throne of God who, *'never cease to say, "Holy, holy, holy, is the Lord God Almighty, who was and is, and is to come!"*
(Revelation chapter 4 verse 8 - ESV)

This level of continuous worship demonstrates heaven's complete awe and passion for the absolute and supreme holiness of God.

In the book of Habakkuk, the prophet calls out to God, *"Your eyes are too pure to look on evil; you cannot tolerate wrongdoing."*
(Habakkuk chapter 1 verse 13 - ESV)

In the book of 1 Samuel, Hannah earnestly prays, *"There is none holy like the Lord: for there is none besides you; there is no rock like our God."*
(1 Samuel chapter 2 verse 2 - ESV)

God exists on the ultimate level of moral purity, which separates him above all other things.

God is holy, holy, holy.

As a Christian, you need lead a holy life.
Being holy means separating yourself from sinful conduct.
Being holy in everything that you do and say and think,

you become a shining example of God's love and power in this world.

Jesus Christ told his believers to, *"let your light shine before others, that they may see your good deeds and glorify your Father in heaven."*
(Matthew chapter 5 verse 16 - NIV)

The Holy Spirit

When you accept Jesus Christ as your Savior, God gives you a gift.

God's gift is his Holy Spirit.

The Holy Spirit enters your being, and fills you with God's peace and love.

When you receive the Holy Spirit, it can feel as if you have been embraced by God.

'We know how dearly God loves us, because he has given us the Holy Spirit to fill our hearts with his love.'
(Romans chapter 5 verse 5 - NLT)

The Holy Spirit is an amazing and wonderful gift.

What is the Holy Spirit?

The Holy Spirit is God.

God exists in three persons: the Father, the Son, and the Holy Spirit.

Let me explain this: -

A long time ago, when Patrick was converting the people of Ireland to Christianity, he was asked to explain how three beings can be one, and how one being can be three.

Patrick plucked a little shamrock leaf that was growing at his feet and held it up for all to see. The shamrock is a little plant with three distinct leaf sections; Patrick asked his listeners to tell him if the shamrock had one leaf or three.

The people replied was that it is both one leaf *and* three.

"And so it is with God," replied Patrick.

Which means that when you become a Christian and receive the Holy Spirit, God truly lives within you.

'If we love each other, God lives in us. His love is made perfect in us. He has given us His Spirit. This is how we live by His help and He lives in us.'

(1 John chapter 4 verses 12 and 13 - NLT)

I was just a boy when I became a Christian.

I didn't know very much about the Bible, or God or Jesus, and I certainly didn't know much about the Holy Spirit.

Realizing my guilt after doing something horribly insulting to another person, I spoke six words of earnest prayer: "God I'm ashamed. Please forgive me."

If I had any idea what was going to happen next I would have found somewhere more appropriate; I was alone, but I was upstairs in a school corridor. Immediately I had spoken that little prayer, something supernatural happened to me.

From the top of my head to the tips of my toes I realized a sensation that felt like someone was pouring warm honey over me; it enveloped me, leaving me completely elated, and more than a little nervous.

I was so overwhelmed by this weird and unexpected sensation that I couldn't feel the floor I was standing on. I could see my feet, and they were definitely on the floor, but I couldn't feel the floor: I felt like I was floating. In most other situations I would have been fine, but I was upstairs in an almost-empty school building (*I had been kept behind for detention, again*), and I had to somehow descend the stairs to make my way home. I must have looked comically drunk, because I grabbed the handrail with both hands and carefully made my way along it, hand-over-fist, cautiously descending the stairs, worried that I might float over the banister rail and crash into the stairwell below.

I have listened to many, many people explain what happened to them when they became a Christian, but I have only ever heard one other believer describe an experienced like mine. I can't explain it - that's just what happened to me.

My introduction to the Holy Spirit may be quite different from your experience, but that's fine - if you experience something different, please don't feel inadequate. Most people testify to experiencing a wonderful sensation of peace, love and inner confidence when they receive the Holy Spirit. Regardless of what we experience, the only thing that really matters is the truth that you have received God's forgiveness, and his Holy Spirit lives within you.

Where is the Holy Spirit?

As a Christian, you can't see the Holy Spirit that lives within you. Your doctor can't examine the Holy Spirit within you. A surgeon can't open you up and give the Holy Spirit a poke.

There is a part of each of us that is not a physical part of our body, but which is a vital part of what makes us who we are as individuals.

It is called our *soul*.

Humans are not just wonderful pieces of biological

engineering; we have personalities that are unique to each one of us.

If you have ever fallen in love, you will know that the feelings you enjoy are not physical, but come from your soul, (usually referred to as your heart - but your heart is just the organ that pumps blood around your body).

You are your soul.

What you see in the mirror, and what your doctor examines, is your body.

You can't actually see your soul, but the condition of your soul is expressed in your facial expressions and attitude, likes and dislikes, (love, hate, anger, happiness, depression, and so on). You know that your soul exists, because your soul is who you are.

When you accept Jesus Christ as your Savior, God gives you his Holy Spirit.

God's Holy Spirit affects your soul and changes your whole outlook on life.

Living as a Christian with the Holy Spirit within you, you will still suffer temptation and trials and times of deep pain and despair, but through all your ups and downs God will remain faithful, loving, and completely true to all of his promises; and his Holy Spirit supports you and bolsters you, and guides you.

'If God himself has taken up residence in your life, you can hardly be thinking more of yourself than of him. Anyone, of course, who has not welcomed this invisible but clearly present God, the Spirit of Christ, won't know what we're talking about. But for you who welcome him, in whom he dwells—even though you still experience all the limitations

of sin—you yourself experience life on God's terms. It stands to reason, doesn't it, that if the alive-and-present God who raised Jesus from the dead moves into your life, he'll do the same thing in you that he did in Jesus, bringing you alive to himself? When God lives and breathes in you (and he does, as surely as he did in Jesus), you are delivered from that dead life. With his Spirit living in you, your body will be as alive as Christ's!'
(Romans chapter 8 verses 9 to 11 - MSG)

'The fruit of the Spirit is love, joy, peace, forbearance, kindness, goodness, faithfulness, gentleness and self-control.' (Galatians chapter 5 verses 22 and 23 - NIV)

Becoming a Christian isn't just about being saved from the condemnation at the Judgment.

Becoming a Christian is a life-changing experience that we can enjoy in our day-to-day lives.

Becoming a Christian means that God is living within you, through his Holy Spirit.

This explains how God knows everything about us.

God knows your worries.

God shares your happiness.

God understands your grief and pain and suffering.

God knows everything that you need before you do.

'The Spirit helps us in our weakness. We do not know what we ought to pray for, but the Spirit himself intercedes for us through wordless groans. And he who searches our hearts knows the mind of the Spirit, because the Spirit intercedes for God's people in accordance with the will of God.'
(Romans chapter 8 verses 26 and 27 - NIV)

The Holy Spirit is God's gift to you when you believe and ask God's forgiveness.

The Holy Spirit is God, living within you.

The Holy Spirit is the proof that God loves you, and that God exists in your life.

'Do you not know that your body is a temple of the Holy Spirit within you, whom you have from God? You are not your own, for you were bought with a price. So glorify God in your body.'
(1 Corinthians chapter 6 verses 19 and 20 - ESV)

The Judgment

There will be a judgment.

Some will have been saved.

Everyone else will be condemned.

The Old Testament predicts the birth of Jesus Christ hundreds of times. God makes promises that he will send a Savior, and the prophets frequently predict his coming throughout the Old Testament.

So, if all of these hundreds of Old Testament predictions have already come true about the birth of Jesus Christ, we need to pay particular attention to the *thousands* of biblical references that point to the second coming of Christ for the Judgment.

When Christ returns he will be the Judge.

My young son giggled at me recently when something I was working on fell apart: he joked, "You must have upset God, and he is punishing you!"

I corrected my son, because that's not how things work any longer: -

In Old Testament times God punished people for their disobedience and wickedness.

Remember in Genesis Chapter 7, how God sent the great flood that wiped out everyone, except for Noah and his family who had obeyed God and built the ark.

Remember in Genesis chapter 19, how God sent total destruction on the wicked cities of Sodom and Gomorrah, killing everyone, except for Lot and his daughters who were urgently dragged to safety by angels.

Remember in Exodus chapters 7 to 12, the series of disasters that God sent on Egypt to persuade the king to release the Israelites from over 400 years of slavery; finally sending the disaster that killed the firstborn man and beast of every household; only the households that were obedient to God's instructions to sacrifice a lamb were passed over.

Remember in 2 Kings chapters 24 and 25, how God allowed the defeat and total destruction of Jerusalem, and allowed the people to be taken into captivity in Babylon for 70 years.

In each of these examples, God was very displeased with the people, and he demonstrated his anger by punishing them with disasters, death, destruction and defeat.

However, that was Old Testament times.
We are now living in New Testament times.

The New Testament delivers a new covenant between God and mankind, a new promise, and a completely new relationship with God.
Now, God does not respond to our wickedness and disobedience by dealing out disasters, destruction and defeat. Instead, God responds to our sin with the offer of forgiveness.

However, when Paul explained how we should examine ourselves before we participate in the Lord's Supper, he delivered a stern warning: *'If you eat the bread or drink the cup without honoring the body of Christ, you are eating and drinking God's judgment upon yourself. That is why many of you are weak and sick and some have even died.*

But if we would examine ourselves, we would not be judged by God in this way. Yet when we are judged by the Lord, we are being disciplined so that we will not be condemned along with the world.' (1 Corinthians chapter 11 verses 29 to 32 - NLT) What this means is that God has prevented some Christians who showed no care about the broken body of Christ, from participating in the Lord's Supper; God is putting them straight now, through illness and even death, so that these people will not need to face condemnation at the Judgment. This is Fatherly love - correcting his children, preventing them from getting into much deeper trouble later on.

"My child, don't make light of the LORD's discipline, and don't give up when he corrects you. For the LORD disciplines those he loves, and he punishes each one he accepts as his child." (Hebrews chapter 12 verses 5 and 6 - NLT)

Why does God respond to sinners with the offer of forgiveness?

The answer is simple: -

Everyone will be punished, except for the people who have realized that they are unworthy sinners and have asked God for forgiveness; God's forgiveness has been made available to us through the sacrifice of God's only Son, Jesus Christ.

When Jesus Christ was killed on the cross, his sacrifice was what God required to forgive our sins, when we believe.

God's New Testament gives us a very simple choice: -
EITHER: Accept that you are a sinner who deserves

God's condemnation, and ask God for forgiveness.

OR: Do not believe in God or the offer of forgiveness that he has freely provided for you, and face God's full condemnation at the Judgment.

The Bible is very clear: Jesus Christ will return

When Jesus Christ returns, he is coming to judge.

If you believe in God, and have asked God to forgive your sins, you will receive his amazing gift of forgiveness and a wonderful new heavenly existence.

However, if you do not believe in God and have neglected to ask for God's forgiveness, when you are judged for your sins you will be found guilty and thrown into the lake of fire where you will suffer forever.

Why has God freely provided you with the true opportunity of forgiveness?

Because God loves you, that's why.

How will Jesus Christ return?

About 2,000 years ago, the Son of God took on human form, and was born as the little baby Jesus so that he could grow up as a human who would be the perfect sacrifice that God required to allow the forgiveness of our sins.

At that time, Jesus had been born into very, very humble and vulnerable circumstances, and his birth had only been announced to some shepherds.

However, when Jesus Christ returns he will not be an unnoticed arrival in the middle of the night.

When Jesus Christ returns, everyone in the whole world will be amazed by his arrival.

"The sun will be darkened, the moon will give no light, the stars will fall from the sky, and the powers in the heavens will be shaken. Then everyone will see the Son of Man [Jesus Christ] coming on the clouds with great power and glory. And he will send out his angels to gather his chosen ones from all over the world—from the farthest ends of the earth and heaven."
(Mark chapter 13 verses 24 to 27 - NLT)

We will all know when Jesus Christ returns to judge; the event will be unmissable headline news: *"you will see the Son of Man (Jesus Christ) seated in the place of power at God's right hand and coming on the clouds of heaven."*
(Mark chapter 14 verse 62 - NLT)

When Jesus Christ returns, the event will be unmistakable and truly awesome.

What will happen when Jesus Christ returns?
The very first thing that will happen, is that the bodies of all true Christian believers who have died will be resurrected from their graves, and raised as spiritual bodies.

'First, the believers who have died will rise from their graves. Then, together with them, we who are still alive and remain on the earth will be caught up in the clouds to meet the Lord in the air. Then we will be with the Lord forever.' (1 Thessalonians chapter 4 verses 16 to 17 - NIV)

Then, joining the resurrected, all Christian believers who are alive when Jesus Christ returns, will be transformed from mortal to immortal, from corruptible to incorruptible.

How's that!

The first thing that will happen when Jesus Christ returns, is that all Christian believers will be taken up to be in heaven with the Lord forever.

What will happen to everyone who is left behind?

Now that it's too late, I guess the first thing to happen is that a lot of people will wish they'd paid attention to the good message of salvation; because once all the Christians have been taken up to heaven, everyone left behind will have to face the Judgment.

Jesus Christ, *'will come with his mighty angels, in flaming fire, bringing judgment on those who don't know God and on those who refuse to obey the Good News of our Lord Jesus. They will be punished with eternal destruction, forever separated from the Lord and from his glorious power. When he comes on that day, he will receive glory from his holy people—praise from all who believe.'*
(2 Thessalonians chapter 1 verses 7 to 10 - NLT)

"When the Son of Man [Jesus Christ] comes in his glory, and all the angels with him, then he will sit upon his glorious throne. All the nations will be gathered in his presence, and he will separate the people as a shepherd separates the sheep from the goats. He will place the sheep at his right hand and the goats at his left.

"Then the King will say to those on his right, 'Come, you who are blessed by my Father, inherit the Kingdom prepared for you from the creation of the world. For I was hungry, and you fed me. I was thirsty, and you gave me a drink. I was a stranger, and you invited me into your home. I was naked, and you gave me clothing. I was sick, and you

cared for me. I was in prison, and you visited me.' "Then these righteous ones will reply, 'Lord, when did we ever see you hungry and feed you? Or thirsty and give you something to drink? Or a stranger and show you hospitality? Or naked and give you clothing? When did we ever see you sick or in prison and visit you?' "And the King will say, 'I tell you the truth, when you did it to one of the least of these my brothers and sisters, you were doing it to me!'

"Then the King will turn to those on the left and say, 'Away with you, you cursed ones, into the eternal fire prepared for the devil and his demons. For I was hungry, and you didn't feed me. I was thirsty, and you didn't give me a drink. I was a stranger, and you didn't invite me into your home. I was naked, and you didn't give me clothing. I was sick and in prison, and you didn't visit me.' "Then they will reply, 'Lord, when did we ever see you hungry or thirsty or a stranger or naked or sick or in prison, and not help you?' "And he will answer, 'I tell you the truth, when you refused to help the least of these my brothers and sisters, you were refusing to help me.' "And they will go away into eternal punishment, but the righteous will go into eternal life."
(Matthew chapter 25 verses 31 to 46 - NLT)

Is that clear enough?

These words, which have been translated directly from the lips of Jesus Christ, clearly state that he will separate us into two groups: -

There will be a group of people who believe in God, and who have lived a life that genuinely demonstrates a caring love and kindness toward others;

And there will be a group of people who have not genuinely demonstrated a caring love and kindness toward others.

The loving, kind group will receive eternal life.

The unloving, unkind group will receive eternal punishment.

Which group of people do you belong to?

How will the Judgment happen?

About 600 years before the birth of Jesus, a vision of the Judgment was revealed to the Old Testament prophet Daniel: *'As I looked, thrones were placed, and the Ancient of Days took his seat; his clothing was white as snow, and the hair of his head like pure wool; his throne was fiery flames; its wheels were burning fire. A stream of fire issued and came out from before him; a thousand thousands served him, and ten thousand times ten thousand stood before him; the court sat in judgment, and the books were opened.'* (Daniel chapter 7 verses 9 and 10 - ESV)

The books were opened!

What books?

'Then I saw a great white throne and him who was seated on it. From his presence earth and sky fled away, and no place was found for them. And I saw the dead, great and small, standing before the throne, and books were opened. Then another book was opened, which is the book of life. And the dead were judged by what was written in the books, according to what they had done. And the sea gave up the dead who were in it, Death and Hades gave up the dead who were in them, and they were judged, each one of them,

according to what they had done. Then Death and Hades were thrown into the lake of fire. This is the second death, the lake of fire. And if anyone's name was not found written in the book of life, he was thrown into the lake of fire.'
(Revelation chapter 20 verses 11 to 15 - ESV)

So, there already exists an account of each one of us, and it is recorded in a book.
What do you think this record will say about you?

How will Jesus Christ judge us?

Jesus Christ, *'will judge everyone according to what they have done. He will give eternal life to those who keep on doing good, seeking after the glory and honor and immortality that God offers. But he will pour out his anger and wrath on those who live for themselves, who refuse to obey the truth and instead live lives of wickedness. There will be trouble and calamity for everyone who keeps on doing what is evil. But there will be glory and honor and peace from God for all who do good.'*
(Romans chapter 2 verses 6 to 10 - NLT)

At the Judgment, Jesus Christ will sort everyone out.
There will be a wonderful new life for people who believe in God and have asked for the forgiveness of their sins. However, Jesus Christ warned that: *"Just as the weeds are sorted out and burned in the fire, so it will be at the end of the world. The Son of Man will send his angels, and they will remove from his Kingdom everything that causes sin and all who do evil. And the angels will throw them into the fiery furnace, where there will be weeping and gnashing of teeth."*
(Matthew chapter 13 verses 40 to 42 - NLT)

Are you ready to be judged?

Jesus Christ delivered a warning that should make you pay attention: *"Do not judge others, and you will not be judged. For you will be treated as you treat others. The standard you use in judging is the standard by which you will be judged."* (Matthew chapter 7 verses 1 and 2 - NLT)

When Jesus Christ taught his disciples the manner in which they should pray, he told them to pray asking God to, *"forgive us our sins, as we have forgiven those who sin against us,"*

And then Jesus warned his disciples that, *"If you forgive those who sin against you, your heavenly Father will forgive you. But if you refuse to forgive others, your Father will not forgive your sins."*

(Matthew chapter 6 verses 12, 14 and 15 - NLT)

You and I, we shall be judged in the same way in which we have judged others.

And we shall be forgiven in the same way in which we have forgiven others.

When will Jesus Christ return to Judge us?

I don't know.

The angels don't know.

Jesus Christ doesn't even know.

"No one knows the day or hour when these things will happen, not even the angels in heaven or the Son himself. Only the Father knows." (Matthew chapter 24 verse 36 - NLT)

Jesus Christ will return to earth to judge everyone at a time that only God knows.

"When the Son of Man returns, it will be like it was in Noah's day. In those days before the flood, the people were enjoying banquets and parties and weddings right up to the time Noah entered his boat. People didn't realize what was going to happen until the flood came and swept them all away. That is the way it will be when the Son of Man comes. Two men will be working together in the field; one will be taken, the other left. Two women will be grinding flour at the mill; one will be taken, the other left.

"So you, too, must keep watch! For you don't know what day your Lord is coming. Understand this: If a homeowner knew exactly when a burglar was coming, he would keep watch and not permit his house to be broken into. You also must be ready all the time, for the Son of Man will come when least expected."

(Matthew chapter 24 verses 37 to 44 - NLT)

Are you ready?

Because, 'a day of anger is coming, when God's righteous judgment will be revealed.'

(Romans chapter 2 verse 5 - NLT)

The Lord's Supper

You might know this as **communion**.

Different churches have different names for this simple but very significant little meal, but in the Bible it is called the **Lord's Supper**, or **Breaking Bread**.

Jesus instructed his disciples to, *"do this in remembrance of me."* (Gospel of Luke chapter 22 verse 19 - KJV)

What is the Lord's Supper all about?

You've maybe seen church members solemnly sharing bread and wine during a service, and perhaps you felt a little uncomfortable, wondering what's going on, (perhaps wondering if you should join in too).

Sharing this special little meal is something you most **definitely should not do** unless you are a committed Christian who fully understands the full meaning of it all.

Paul explains the consequences of participating in the Lord's Supper if you are not fully aware of what you are taking part in, warning that, *'whoever eats the bread or drinks the cup of the Lord in an unworthy manner will be guilty of sinning against the body and blood of the Lord. Everyone ought to examine themselves before they eat of the bread and drink from the cup. For those who eat and drink without discerning the body of Christ eat and drink judgment on themselves.'*
(1 Corinthians chapter 11 verses 27 to 29 - NIV)

You definitely don't want to risk God's judgment, so we need to realize what the Lord's Supper is all about.

To understand the Lord's Supper, you need to understand the Passover

The Passover and the Lord's Supper are completely different ceremonies, but you can't fully understand the significance of the Lord's Supper until you understand what the Passover was all about.

The Passover was remembered every year on the anniversary of the occasion when God's chosen people were spared from the curse of death that was poured out over Egypt; the Passover delivered freedom to God's chosen people.

On the night when Jesus knew he was going to be arrested and taken away for trial and execution, it was not a coincidence that this occurred during the annual Passover celebration.

Jesus and his disciples prepared for their Passover meal in an upstairs room in Jerusalem. However, this was not to be a repeat of Passover meal that their ancestors had observed for almost 1,500 years; this was to be the last supper they would enjoy in the company of Jesus Christ before his crucifixion.

Because Jesus was about to change everything.

Some people call this the Last Supper.

Perhaps it should be called the First Supper.

The annual ritual meal of the Passover had been celebrated every year since Moses led the Israelites out of Egypt. The Passover meal had a strict format: a Passover lamb had to be sacrificed; the head of the house would speak the words that were recited every Passover; they would share the bread, and they would share the wine.

At this last supper, Jesus naturally assumed the position of head of the house to lead the ritual of the Passover meal.

But instead of reciting the traditional words of the Passover, Jesus took the bread, and when he had given thanks to God, he broke it and gave it to his disciples, and said, *"Take this and eat it, for this is my body.*
(Matthew chapter 26 verse 26 - NLT)

This is the moment when everything changed - this meal was no longer a Passover meal.

Jesus Christ was changing everything, forever.

Can you imagine how confused his disciples must have been?

Jesus took the cup of wine, and when he had given thanks he passed it to his disciples, saying, *"Each of you drink from it, for this is my blood, which confirms the covenant between God and his people. It is poured out as a sacrifice to forgive the sins of many."*
(Matthew chapter 26 verses 27 and 28 - NIV)

These close friends of Jesus had no idea of the events that were about to take place, but Jesus knew.

Jesus knew that one of his closest friends was about to betray him; Jesus knew that he would soon be arrested, humiliated, punished, and horribly executed.

The Old Testament Passover ritual required a sacrificial lamb. Jesus would give his body, symbolized by the bread.

Jesus would give his blood, symbolized by the wine.
Jesus would be the sacrificial lamb of the New Testament.   Jesus Christ is the Lamb of God.

The sacrifice that Jesus was going to suffer on the cross would change everything.
The old Passover meal was shared in remembrance of the freedom of the Israelites from slavery in Egypt.
The Lord's Supper replaces that Old Testament ritual.
The Lord's Supper is shared in remembrance of the sacrifice that Jesus Christ suffered to free believers from their slavery to sin.

As a Christian, you can participate in the Lord's Supper.
'The Lord Jesus, on the night he was betrayed, took bread, and when he had given thanks, he broke it and said, "This is my body, which is for you; do this in remembrance of me." In the same way, after supper he took the cup, saying, "This cup is the new covenant in my blood; do this, whenever you drink it, in remembrance of me." For whenever you eat this bread and drink this cup, you proclaim the Lord's death until he comes.' (1 Corinthians chapter 11 verses 23 to 26 - ESV)

Participating in the Lord's Supper is a serious and solemn act of remembrance.
Participating in the Lord's Supper, we remember the old Passover meal that celebrated the freedom from slavery of the Israelites so long ago.
Participating in the Lord's Supper, we realize that the Passover lamb has been replaced by the body and blood of Jesus Christ.
Participating in the Lord's Supper, we are solemnly

remembering the sacrifice that Jesus made on our behalf, which has bought us freedom from our slavery to sin, and which has made us acceptable to God.

As a Christian it is very important that you examine your motives for participating in the Lord's Supper: test your heart, and accept the bread and wine with the deepest respect for the sacrifice that Jesus Christ made for you.

To really focus your mind during the Lord's Supper, think of your sins: think of the secret things you have done or said or thought that you are truly, deeply ashamed of.

Now, realize that the punishment for these things has been laid on Jesus Christ.

Jesus Christ has accepted the punishment that you rightly deserve.

Take the bread and realize that the body of Jesus Christ has been given as the sacrifice that has released you from the responsibility of your sins.

Take the wine and realize that the blood of Jesus Christ was spilt from his brutalized body when he accepted the punishment that you deserve for your sins.

When you participate in the Lord's Supper, remember, remember, remember: Jesus Christ gave himself so that your sins can be forgiven; through the sacrifice that Jesus Christ made on the cross, you can make yourself acceptable in God's sight.

Such a sacrifice demands our deepest and most solemn respect.

'Anyone who eats the bread or drinks the cup of the Master irreverently is like part of the crowd that jeered and spit on him at his death. Is that the kind of "remembrance" you want to be part of? Examine your motives, test your heart, come to this meal in holy awe.'

(1 Corinthians chapter 11 verse 29 - MSG)

The Old Testament and the New Testament

To understand the true significance of the New Testament you need to understand the Old Testament.

The word *Testament* is the English translation of the Greek word *Diatheke*, which can be interpreted as, *a covenant or a binding agreement*.

In this respect you can read the Old Testament and the New Testament as, the Old Agreement and the New Agreement: the Old Agreement was made between God and the people of Israel; and the New Agreement was made between God and all people, which has allowed everyone who has asked God for forgiveness to be forgiven.

As with any covenant or binding agreement, there are legalities: there are rules that must be observed for the contract to be fulfilled.

Let me explain it as a banking agreement: -

If you need to borrow money, you might go to a bank and ask for a loan.

If the bank agrees to lend you money, there would be a legal agreement between you and the bank to ensure that you repay the loan. However, this agreement will be one-sided because you will owe the bank the money, but the bank will owe you nothing. In other words, the bank makes the conditions of the loan because it is the lender; as the borrower, it is up to you to meet the conditions demanded by the lender.

This is an example of a binding agreement, or a covenant.

What is the Old Testament all about?

The first five books of the Bible were written by Moses. These are: **Genesis**, **Exodus**, **Leviticus**, **Numbers**, and **Deuteronomy**. These five books deliver the instructions that God gave to Moses, and are often referred to as *the Law of Moses*.

In the book of **Exodus**, God gave a long series of conditions for Moses to deliver to the Israelites, beginning with the ten commandments.

This list of commandments can be found in the book of Exodus chapters 20, 21, 22, and 23.

'Moses went down to the people and repeated all the instructions and regulations the Lord had given him. All the people answered with one voice, "We will do everything the Lord has commanded." Then Moses carefully wrote down all the Lord's instructions. Early the next morning Moses got up and built an altar at the foot of the mountain. He also set up twelve pillars, one for each of the twelve tribes of Israel. Then he sent some of the young Israelite men to present burnt offerings and to sacrifice bulls as peace offerings to the Lord. Moses drained half the blood from these animals into basins. The other half he splattered against the altar. Then he took the Book of the Covenant and read it aloud to the people. Again they all responded, "We will do everything the Lord has commanded. We will obey." Then Moses took the blood from the basins and splattered it over the people, declaring, "Look, this blood confirms the cove-

nant the Lord has made with you in giving you these in-structions." (Exodus chapter 24 verses 3 to 7 - NLT)

In return for meeting the conditions of the covenant that God made with the Israelites, God promised to give them the land of Canaan, which is described as a land flowing with milk and honey.
Because God had made this covenant with the Israelites, the land of Canaan is called the Promised Land.

The ups and downs of the descendants of these Israelites, and their sporadic obedience and frequent disobedience to God's covenant is described in the Old Testament books of **Joshua**, **Judges**, **Ruth**, **1 Samuel**, **2 Samuel**, **1 Kings**, **2 Kings**, **1 Chronicles**, **2 Chronicles**, **Ezra**, **Nehemiah**, and **Ester**.

The book of **Joshua** describes the seven-year conquest of the land of Canaan, and the partitioning of the land between the tribes of Israel.

The book of **Judges** describes a difficult period. The Israelites had not chased out all of the original inhabitants of Canaan, and some Israelites had adopted the worship of false gods. God raised up heroes (the judges) to deliver God's people from the oppression of their enemies.

The book of **Ruth** describes the circumstances and salvation of Ruth; this book illustrates acceptance, righteousness, love and faithfulness.

The first book of **Samuel** describes the establishment of the Israelite monarchy and the rulership of Saul, their first king.

The second book of **Samuel** describes the appointment and reign of Israel's most famous ruler, King David.

The first and second books of **Kings** describe a divided kingdom after the death of King Solomon: ten tribes become the northern kingdom of Israel; the remaining two tribes of Benjamin and Judah become the southern kingdom of Judah. All of the kings of Israel were bad, and their land was conquered by the Assyrians. Twelve of the twenty rulers of Judah were bad, and they were ultimately conquered; Jerusalem and the temple that Solomon had built were completely destroyed, and the important people were all taken into 70 years' captivity in Babylon.

The first and second books of **Chronicles** retell the history of David and the subsequent kings of Judah.

The books of **Ezra** and **Nehemiah** describe the return of the people to their destroyed homeland from 70 years' captivity in Babylon. Jerusalem is rebuilt and repopulated, illustrating God's forgiveness, and his power to restore.

The book of **Esther** describes the remarkable story of Esther who risked everything to stop the Persian genocide of all of the Jews who had been living in captivity in Babylon, and had come under the control of Persia when Babylon was conquered.

Throughout the Biblical history of Israel and Judah, the people lived under the covenant of the law that God had given them through Moses in the first five books of the Bible.

However, the people had frequently failed to fulfill their side of their covenant with God, and as a result they suffered the consequences with invasions by neighboring countries, captivity, and the destruction of their most important city, Jerusalem.

Another major section of the Old Testament is made up of 17 books written by 16 different prophets of God.

A prophet was a person who had been chosen by God as his personal spokesperson and messenger.

God delivered his message to the prophets, and the prophets delivered these messages to the people on God's behalf.

These Old Testament books of the prophets are: **Isaiah**, **Jeremiah**, **Lamentations** (which was written by Jeremiah), **Ezekiel**, **Daniel**, **Hosea**, **Joel**, **Amos**, **Obadiah**, **Jonah**, **Micah**, **Nahum**, **Habakkuk**, **Zephaniah**, **Haggai**, **Zechariah**, and **Malachi**.

Each of these books of the prophets is important.

God had spent centuries preparing the way for the coming of Jesus Christ. God prepared the way for the arrival of our Savior by repeatedly giving advanced notice of his coming through a succession of prophets.

The prophets specified how Jesus Christ would be born to a virgin;

The prophets specified the place where Jesus Christ would be born;

The prophets predicted the message of good news that Jesus Christ would deliver to the world;

And the prophets told of the reconciliation that Jesus Christ would make between God and mankind.

The prophet Jeremiah declared that: *"The day is coming,"* says the LORD, *"when I will make a new covenant with the people of Israel and Judah. This covenant will not be like the one I made with their ancestors when I took them by the hand and brought them out of the land of Egypt. They broke that covenant, though I loved them as a husband loves his wife," says the LORD.*

"But this is the new covenant I will make with the people of Israel after those days," says the LORD. "I will put my instructions deep within them, and I will write them on their hearts. I will be their God, and they will be my people. And they will not need to teach their neighbors, nor will they need to teach their relatives, saying, 'You should know the LORD.' For everyone, from the least to the greatest, will know me already," says the LORD. "And I will forgive their wickedness, and I will never again remember their sins." (Jeremiah chapter 31 verses 31 to 34 - NLT)

Here, Jeremiah is stating that the old covenant will be replaced. Jeremiah is stating that there will be a new covenant and a new relationship with God.

This new covenant is declared in the first sentence of the New Testament.

How does the New Testament prove the fulfillment of the new covenant?

The very first sentence of the New Testament simply states: *'The book of the genealogy of Jesus Christ, the son of David, the son of Abraham.'* (Matthew chapter 1 verse 1 - ESV) This statement is followed by a long list of ancestors in direct line from Abraham to Jesus.

What does this statement mean?

About 1,000 years before the birth of Jesus Christ, God made a promise to David: *'I will raise up one of your descendants, your own offspring, and I will make his kingdom strong. He is the one who will build a house—a temple—for my name. And I will secure his royal throne forever. I will be his father, and he will be my son.'*
(2 Samuel chapter 7 verses 12 to 14 - NIV)

About 1,900 years before the birth of Jesus Christ, God told Abram that, *"All nations will be blessed through you."*
(Genesis chapter 12 verse 3 - NIV)

The opening sentence of the New Testament is clearly stating that this descendant of Abram, through whom *all nations will be blessed*, has arrived.

That same opening statement of the New Testament is clearly stating that this descendant of David, *who will build a temple for God's name*, has arrived.

This opening sentence of the New Testament is stating that Jesus is the long-awaited Savior of the world, the Messiah, the Christ, the Chosen One.

Over and over again throughout his life, Jesus made it clear in his actions and teachings that he was fulfilling all the prophesies of the Old Testament.

It was very important that Jesus fulfilled all these prophesies, because this validates who he is: it proves that Jesus is the Christ, Jesus is the Messiah, Jesus is the person whom God sent to save the world from sin.

When Jesus Christ appeared to his disciples after his death and resurrection, he explained to his disciples: *"When I was with you before, I told you that everything written about me in the law of Moses and the prophets and in the Psalms must be fulfilled." Then he opened their minds to understand the Scriptures. And he said, "Yes, it was written long ago that the Messiah would suffer and die and rise from the dead on the third day. It was also written that this message would be proclaimed in the authority of his name to all the nations, beginning in Jerusalem: 'There is forgiveness of sins for all who repent.' You are witnesses of all these things."*

(Luke chapter 24 verses 44 to 48 - NLT)

How did Jesus Christ deliver a new covenant?

In his letter to the Hebrews, Paul briefly described the Old Testament rituals, regulations and rigmarole required for worshiping God.

Paul explained how the old system and the High Priest of the Tabernacle has been replaced: *'Christ has now become the High Priest over all the good things that have come. He has entered that greater, more perfect Tabernacle in heaven, which was not made by human hands and is not part of this created world. With his own blood—not the blood of goats and calves—he entered the Most Holy Place once for all time and secured our redemption forever. Under the old system, the blood of goats and bulls and the ashes of a heifer could cleanse people's bodies from ceremonial impurity. Just think how much more the blood of Christ will purify our consciences from sinful deeds so that we can worship the living God. For by the power of the eternal Spirit, Christ offered himself to God as a perfect sacrifice for our sins. That is why he is the one who mediates a new covenant between God and people, so that all who are called can receive the eternal inheritance God has promised them. For Christ died to set them free from the penalty of the sins they had committed under that first covenant.'* (Hebrews chapter 9 verses 11 to 15 - NLT)

The conditions of the old covenant with God required strict obedience to all of God's laws. And because the people kept sinning, they had to keep making animal sacrifices to keep compensating God for their sins.

God's plan provided the perfect sacrifice that was the sacrifice to end all sacrifices for the forgiveness of sins.

The perfect sacrifice that God provided to achieve this once-and-forever forgiveness of sins was his only Son, Jesus Christ.

"God so loved the world that he gave his one and only Son, that whoever believes in him shall not perish but have eternal life. For God did not send his Son into the world to condemn the world, but to save the world through him." (John chapter 3 verses 16 and 17 - NIV)

Jesus Christ is the new go-between between God and mankind. In the Old Testament the go-between was a High Priest. Now, with the new covenant, Jesus Christ is the High Priest.

'There were many priests under the old system, for death prevented them from remaining in office. But because Jesus lives forever, his priesthood lasts forever. Therefore he is able, once and forever, to save those who come to God through him. He lives forever to intercede with God on their behalf. He is the kind of high priest we need because he is holy and blameless, unstained by sin. He has been set apart from sinners and has been given the highest place of

honor in heaven. Unlike those other high priests, he does not need to offer sacrifices every day. They did this for their own sins first and then for the sins of the people. But Jesus did this once for all when he offered himself as the sacrifice for the people's sins. The law appointed high priests who were limited by human weakness. But after the law was given, God appointed his Son with an oath, and his Son has been made the perfect High Priest forever.'
(Hebrews chapter 7 verses 23 to 28 - NLT)

'Under the old covenant, the priest stands and ministers before the altar day after day, offering the same sacrifices again and again, which can never take away sins. But our High Priest offered himself to God as a single sacrifice for sins, good for all time. Then he sat down in the place of honor at God's right hand. There he waits until his enemies are humbled and made a footstool under his feet. For by that one offering he forever made perfect those who are being made holy."   (Hebrews chapter 10 verses 11 to 14 - NLT)

What is our new covenant with God?

Jesus Christ was the perfect sacrifice that God needed to allow him to forgive your sins.

God can forgive your sins because Jesus Christ has already accepted the punishment for your sins when he was crucified.

'When we were utterly helpless, Christ came at just the right time and died for us sinners. Now, most people would not be willing to die for an upright person, though someone might perhaps be willing to die for a person who is especially good. But God showed his great love for us by sending

Christ to die for us while we were still sinners. And since we have been made right in God's sight by the blood of Christ, he will certainly save us from God's condemnation. For since our friendship with God was restored by the death of his Son while we were still his enemies, we will certainly be saved through the life of his Son. So now we can rejoice in our wonderful new relationship with God because our Lord Jesus Christ has made us friends of God.'
(Romans chapter 5 verses 6 to 11 - NLT)

Let me explain it as a banking agreement again: -

Let's say that you have borrowed a large amount of money from the bank. But you have borrowed more money than you can ever hope to repay. It is impossible for you to fulfill your side of the loan agreement.

You are in deep financial trouble.

Usually, when a bank lends money, the bank requires a **guarantor** for the loan. This means that if you cannot repay the loan, your guarantor is responsible for paying the loan on your behalf; this protects the bank from losing their money.

With the new covenant, your guarantor is Jesus Christ.

If your sin is represented by a huge debt of money, Jesus Christ has already paid off everything on your behalf: Jesus Christ has cleared your debt.

When you ask God to forgive you, the debt of your sins that was impossible for you to repay has been paid on your behalf by Jesus Christ: your sins are forgiven.

And because your sins are forgiven, you will not be condemned to the lake of fire at the Judgment. This means that you can look forward to a new and glorious eternal life in the presence of God.

'God is so rich in mercy, and he loved us so much, that even though we were dead because of our sins, he gave us life when he raised Christ from the dead. (It is only by God's grace that you have been saved!) For he raised us from the dead along with Christ and seated us with him in the heavenly realms because we are united with Christ Jesus. So God can point to us in all future ages as examples of the incredible wealth of his grace and kindness toward us, as shown in all he has done for us who are united with Christ Jesus.

God saved you by his grace when you believed. And you can't take credit for this; it is a gift from God. Salvation is not a reward for the good things we have done, so none of us can boast about it. God's mercy is so abundant, and his love for us is so great, that while we were spiritually dead in our disobedience he brought us to life with Christ. It is by God's grace that you have been saved. In our union with Christ Jesus he raised us up with him to rule with him in the heavenly world. He did this to demonstrate for all time to come the extraordinary greatness of his grace in the love he showed us in Christ Jesus. For it is by God's grace that you have been saved through faith. It is not the result of your own efforts, but God's gift, so that no one can boast about it.' (Ephesians chapter 2 verses 4 to 9 - NLT)

How was this new covenant implemented?

'Jesus and the apostles sat down together at the table. Jesus said, "I have been very eager to eat this Passover meal with you before my suffering begins. For I tell you now that I won't eat this meal again until its meaning is fulfilled in

the Kingdom of God." Then he took a cup of wine and gave thanks to God for it. Then he said, "Take this and share it among yourselves. For I will not drink wine again until the Kingdom of God has come." He took some bread and gave thanks to God for it. Then he broke it in pieces and gave it to the disciples, saying, "This is my body, which is given for you. Do this in remembrance of me." After supper he took another cup of wine and said, "This cup is the new covenant between God and his people—an agreement confirmed with my blood, which is poured out as a sacrifice for you."
(Luke chapter 22 verses 14 to 20 - NLT)

Jesus was killed during the annual remembrance of the Passover.

The original Passover required an unblemished lamb to be sacrificed; by sacrificing a lamb, the Israelites had been saved from the judgment of death that God dealt to Egypt.

When John the Baptist first recognized Jesus Christ, *'John saw Jesus coming toward him and said, "Look! The Lamb of God who takes away the sin of the world!"*
(John chapter 1 verse 29 - NLT)

The new covenant was established by the sacrifice of Jesus Christ in the cross.

'Christ arrives right on time to make this happen. He didn't, and doesn't, wait for us to get ready. He presented himself for this sacrificial death when we were far too weak and rebellious to do anything to get ourselves ready. And even if we hadn't been so weak, we wouldn't have known what to do anyway. We can understand someone dying for a person worth dying for, and we can understand how

*someone good and noble could inspire us to selfless sacrifice.
But God put his love on the line for us by offering his Son in
sacrificial death while we were of no use whatever to him.
Now that we are set right with God by means of this sacrificial death, the consummate blood sacrifice, there is no
longer a question of being at odds with God in any way. If,
when we were at our worst, we were put on friendly terms
with God by the sacrificial death of his Son, now that we're
at our best, just think of how our lives will expand and
deepen by means of his resurrection life! Now that we have
actually received this amazing friendship with God, we are
no longer content to simply say it in plodding prose. We
sing and shout our praises to God through Jesus, the Messiah!'* (Romans chapter 5 verses 6 to 11 - MSG)

The old covenant only existed between God and his
chosen people, the Jews.
The old covenant required the Jews to follow the strict
laws that God had delivered to them through Moses.

The new covenant replaces that old covenant.
The new covenant is a completely new agreement
between God and *all* of mankind, (not just Jewish
people). The new covenant offers everyone the opportunity of a personal relationship with God.

With the new covenant there are no rituals, regulations
and rigmarole required to worship God; there is no
obligation for men to be circumcised; there is no need
to approach God through the high priest at the temple;
there is no need to continually make animal sacrifices
to compensate for our continual sins.

The only requirement is: to believe.

'If you declare with your mouth, "Jesus is Lord," and believe in your heart that God raised him from the dead, you will be saved. For it is with your heart that you believe and are justified, and it is with your mouth that you profess your faith and are saved.'

(Romans chapter 10 verse 10 and 11 - NIV)

The Passover

Although Christians do not observe the Passover, it is important to understand what this remembrance was, because the principles of the Passover directly relate to the sacrifice that Jesus Christ made when he was executed on the cross.

You can read about the Passover in the book of Exodus, chapters 11 and 12.

The Passover is what it says it is: it is when God's judgment safely *passed over* the houses of the people who were obedient to God's instructions.

About 1,500 years before Jesus was born, God's chosen people, the Israelites, were living as slaves under the rule of the Egyptians. They had been slaves for over 400 years.

God appointed Moses to speak on his behalf, instructing him to tell the Egyptian king to, "Let my people go."

Slaves were very important to the Egyptians, slaves did all the hard work, and as you might expect, the King of Egypt said, "No!"

Each time the king said "No!" God sent a curse over Egypt.

The first time the king said "No!" God turned all the water into blood.

The second time, God sent a plague of frogs

The third time, a plague of lice

Then flies

Then a disease that killed their livestock

Then a plague of boils
Thunderstorms of hail and fire
Then a plague of locusts
Then God sent darkness for three full days.
But even after these nine terrible disasters, the king of Egypt still said, "No! They cannot go."

God told Moses that he would bring a tenth disaster over Egypt, a disaster so terrible that the king would definitely let God's chosen people go.

Again, Moses relayed God's message to the king of Egypt. Moses told the king that God would go throughout the whole of Egypt and kill the firstborn of every household.

The king of Egypt was very angry at this threat, and still refused to let God's chosen people go.

God gave strict instructions to Moses, which all of his chosen people had to follow so that this final disaster would safely pass over them: -

On the tenth day of that month, each household had to select a healthy one-year-old male lamb that was without any scars or injuries, and separate this lamb from the other sheep and goats of the flock.

After sunset on the fourteenth day, the lamb must be killed. The lamb must be killed by cutting its neck, and letting it quietly bleed to death.

The blood from the lamb must be used to paint around the front door of each house in which the lamb will be eaten; the blood must be smeared up one side of the doorway, across the top, and down the other side.

That same night, the people of the household must roast the lamb over the fire, and they must eat it with bitter herbs and bread made without yeast.

They must not eat any of the lamb raw or boiled in water: it all must be roasted over the fire, including the head, the legs and all its inner parts.

The people must be fully dressed when they eat the lamb, wearing their sandals, and holding their stick in their hand; and they must eat the lamb quickly.

Any lamb that is left uneaten must be burnt away completely in the fire so that there is nothing left by the time the sun comes up.

God explained that he would pass over the houses marked with the blood of the lamb: no one in the houses marked with the blood of the lamb would be harmed.

But at every house that did not have blood smeared across the door, and who had not followed God's instructions: the firstborn of that household would die.

As sure as God's word, that's what happened. On that night, death visited every household in all of Egypt; but only the homes that had been marked with the blood of the lamb were passed over and saved from death.

That night a terrible cry was heard all over Egypt as the firstborn died in the houses that had not obeyed God's instructions; even the King of Egypt's eldest child had died.

And just as God had predicted, the King of Egypt told Moses to take God's chosen people away, *immediately*.

God told Moses to remember the Passover and celebrate it every year, forever. And it is still celebrated by
Jewish people today, remembering how God released
their ancestors from slavery.

In the **New Testament** you can read that Jesus knew
he would be betrayed and handed over for execution
during the annual remembrance of the Passover.
On the night when Jesus would be arrested, he and his
closest friends shared a Passover meal that changed
everything.
This was the last supper that Jesus would have with his
disciples before he would be crucified.

The fact that Jesus was arrested during the remembrance of the Passover is highly significant.
Let me explain: -
Every time that you read about the Lamb of God, or
when you see a reference to the Lamb written with a
capital 'L', this is not referring to any old lamb, or even
the lamb of the Passover in the time of Moses: this
Lamb with a capital 'L' refers directly to Jesus Christ,
the Son of God.

Why is Jesus Christ called the Lamb of God?

Way back in the time of Moses, God sent the curse of
death over the whole land of Egypt because the King of
Egypt refused to give freedom to God's chosen people.
Through Moses, God told his chosen people that the
only way that they could be saved from this curse of
death was to follow his strict instructions: Sacrifice the
unblemished lamb; Paint their doorframe with the

blood of the lamb; Cook the whole lamb over an open fire; Eat it, and burn away the remains completely.

Only if they followed these instructions would the households be passed over and saved from the death of their firstborn.

However, in the New Testament, a very special sacrifice is required by God to save all sinners from condemnation; but this time an unblemished one-year old sheep wasn't going to be enough for such an amazing gift of forgiveness.

This time, God wasn't just offering protection from death to the Jewish people: **God was offering the forgiveness of sins and the promise of eternal life to everyone who believes in him**.

For this reason, the sacrifice had to be incredibly special, and there was nothing more special to God than his only Son.

"God so loved the world, that he gave his only Son, that whoever believes in him should not perish but have eternal life." (John chapter 3 verse 16 - ESV)

Jesus Christ is the sacrifice that has replaced the lamb of the Passover.

The Passover has been replaced with a new promise from God, which saves all believers from condemnation.

When John the Baptist first recognized Jesus Christ, he exclaimed, *"Behold the Lamb of God, which taketh away the sin of the world."* (John chapter 1 verse 29 - KJV)

Jesus Christ was executed by the cruel death of being

nailed to a cross and left to die; Jesus accepted this horrible death because he knew that this was the only way that the sins of the world can be forgiven by God.

'Christ, our Passover lamb, has been sacrificed.'
(1 Corinthians chapter 5 verse 7 - ESV)

The Passover happened such a long time ago, but it remains important to understand how that sacrifice that freed the Israelites from slavery mirrors the sacrifice that Jesus Christ made, which has freed us from our sins when we believe. If Jesus Christ had not been sacrificed, we could never hope to achieve God's forgiveness for our sins.

Jesus Christ was the Lamb of God.

'And walk in love, as Christ loved us and gave himself up for us, a fragrant offering and sacrifice to God.'
(Ephesians chapter 5 verse 2 - ESV)

Paul, and his letters

Paul was an *apostle*, which is an old Greek word that means that he was an envoy appointed by Jesus Christ.

Paul wrote several very important letters to some of the very first Christian communities. What Paul explains in these letters is still very relevant to Christians today, because the information that Paul provided was directly inspired by his personal encounter with the resurrected Jesus Christ.

The amazing thing about Paul is that he was actively hunting and persecuting Christians right up to the moment when he had an encounter with Jesus Christ. Paul even admits to passively watching a Christian worker called Stephen being stoned to death for believing in Christ.

Before Paul met Jesus and was totally converted to Christianity, Paul's name was Saul.
Saul was Jewish, and he was a Pharisee, (which is an important Jew with much more influence, and a responsibility for keeping other Jews true to the Jewish faith). Saul's job was to hunt Jews who had abandoned the Jewish faith to become Christians.
"I persecuted the followers of this Way [the Christian way] *to their death, arresting both men and women and throwing them into prison"*
(Acts chapter 2 verse 4 - NIV)

Saul was determined in his mission to persecute Christians. Saul went to the High Priest to get an arrest warrant to take to the city of Damascus in Syria; this warrant gave Saul the authority to arrest Christians and take them to Jerusalem to be punished.

However, as he approached Damascus, Saul had an encounter that completely changed his life.

Saul met Jesus Christ.

Meeting Jesus Christ would have been amazing anyway, but this meeting was even more amazing because Jesus had been killed some time earlier.

A bright, bright light suddenly shone all around Saul, and stopped him in his tracks; a voice from the light asked, *"Saul, Saul, why are you persecuting me?"* Saul replied, *"Who are you, Lord?"* And the voice said, *"I am Jesus, whom you are persecuting."*

(Acts chapter 9 verses 4 and 5 - NIV)

Many years after his amazing encounter with the risen Christ, Saul was still overawed by his experience. *'I was caught up to the third heaven fourteen years ago. Whether I was in my body or out of my body, I don't know—only God knows. Yes, only God knows whether I was in my body or outside my body. But I do know that I was caught up to paradise and heard things so astounding that they cannot be expressed in words, things no human is allowed to tell.'*

(2 Corinthians chapter 12 verses 2 to 4 - NLT)

Well, as you'd expect after such an amazing personal encounter with the actual risen Christ, Saul was completely and absolutely converted in his belief to the truth of the good message of Jesus Christ.

It was undeniable: Jesus was the Son of God, and the stories that the Christians were spreading about Jesus being raised from death and returning to heaven were all absolutely true.

'For I would have you know, brothers, that the gospel that was preached by me is not man's gospel. For I did not receive it from any man, nor was I taught it, but I received it through a revelation of Jesus Christ.'

(Galatians chapter 1 verses 11 and 12 - NIV)

Saul, or Paul?

In the book of Acts chapter 13 verse 9, it reads, *"But Saul, who was also called Paul,..."* and from this point in the Bible, Saul is only called *Paul*.

Why so?

Saul had been as born a Roman citizen, and this status was a valuable privilege in those times because Rome ruled this part of the world; however, as a very enthusiastic Pharisee and persecutor of Christians, he had used the Hebrew version of his name, which was *Saul*. But after he was converted in his belief to the truth of the good message of Jesus Christ, he stopped using the Hebrew version of his name, and only ever used the Roman version, *Paul*.

Perhaps Paul made this name change to distance himself from being such an enthusiastic Jew; it also meant that people who were not Jews would not immediately identify him as a Jew, which made him more approachable, because Paul's message was as important to non-Jews as it is to Jews.

Saul adopted the Roman version of his name, and for the rest of the Bible he is only referred to as *Paul*.

Paul travelled extensively in his work for God, educating the early Christian churches in places we recognize today as Syria, Israel, Palestine, Jordan, Turkey, Greece, Cyprus, Malta, and Italy.

Paul wrote many letters to the churches in these different places, which you can read in your Bible.

Paul's letter to the Christian community in Rome, the capital city of modern-day Italy, is called **Romans**.

Paul's letters to the Christian community in Corinth, a city near Athens in Greece, are called **1 Corinthians** and **2 Corinthians**.

Paul's letter to the Christian community in Galatia, an area in modern-day North Eastern Turkey, is called **Galatians**.

Paul's letter to the Christian community in Ephesus, a city on the West coast of modern-day Turkey, is called **Ephesians**.

Paul's letter to the Christian community in Philippi, a city on the North Eastern coast of modern-day Greece, is called **Philippians**.

Paul's letter to the Christian community in Colossae, an inland city in the West of modern-day Turkey, is called **Colossians**.

Paul's letters to the Christian community in Thessaloniki, a city on the coast of Northern Greece, are called **1 Thessalonians** and **2 Thessalonians**.

Paul wrote a letter to the people who had converted from the Jewish faith to Christianity, called **Hebrews**.

And Paul wrote two letters to **Timothy**, a letter to **Titus**, and another to **Philemon**, all of whom were important workers in the early Christian church.

In some of his letters, Paul is clearly very frustrated and expresses his annoyance with the way in which people are misinterpreting Christian principles; and in some letters he is sending messages of encouragement and support.

In all of his letters, Paul educates us and corrects us.

Paul's letters remain very important today.

There is lots of essential information in his letters.

Perhaps one of the most important subjects that Paul explained is that the old, Old Testament relationship that people had with God has completely changed: now there is a new covenant, a New Testament, and a completely new relationship with God, which everyone can enjoy when they believe.

The old Jewish rituals and laws of the Old Testament are no longer relevant; Paul explained that the crucifixion and subsequent resurrection of Jesus Christ, has triggered a fundamental change in our relationship with God: now we can enjoy a relationship with God that is built on faith, not obedience to Old Testament laws.

Paul explained that anyone can be made clean from their sinfulness because of the sacrifice that Jesus Christ made on our behalf.

'God, who is rich in mercy, made us alive with Christ even when we were dead in transgressions - it is by grace you have been saved. And God raised us up with Christ and seated us with him in the heavenly realms in Christ Jesus, in order that in the coming ages he might show the incom-

parable riches of his grace, expressed in his kindness to us in Christ Jesus.

For it is by grace you have been saved, through faith - and this is not from yourselves, it is the gift of God - not by works, so that no one can boast.'

(Ephesians chapter 2 verses 4 to 9 - NIV)

Prayer

Have you ever tried to have a few words of conversation with the Queen of England? Or have you ever tried phoning the President of the United States of America for a chat? It would be very, very difficult for an ordinary person like you or me to get to speak with someone as important as that.

But when we want to speak with the holy, holy, holy Lord God Almighty, it is very, very simple. Praying is our personal direct line of communication with God.

Jesus Christ gave some expert advice on the matter of prayer: *"Here's what I want you to do: Find a quiet, secluded place so you won't be tempted to role-play before God. Just be there as simply and honestly as you can manage. The focus will shift from you to God, and you will begin to sense his grace."* (Matthew chapter 6 verse 6 - MSG)

Prayer is not complicated, but if you feel uncertain about prayer, you are not alone: even the disciples of Jesus asked, *"Lord, teach us to pray..."*
(Luke chapter 11 verse 1 - NIV)

Jesus taught his disciples to pray, addressing God as, *"Our Father,..."*
Jesus has authorized us to address God as our *Father*, so don't feel intimidated by the fact that you are speaking with the Lord God Almighty: when you pray to God, you are praying to a person who loves you as his own child.

Praying develops your relationship with God; speaking

with God regularly, we grow in confidence, faith, and understanding; and we increase our strength and courage to endure difficulties.

Just as speaking with a close friend can be a source of comfort and support, speaking with God is a great source of confidence and solace.

There are lots of examples of prayers in the Bible. The book of Psalms is a great place to understand people's relationship with God and how they communicate with him in good times and bad times. Have a look through the book of Psalms to see how David and other writers approach God and express themselves in their different moods and circumstances.

In 1 Samuel chapter 1, Hannah earnestly prayed to have a son: her lips were moving and tears ran down her face; the priest thought that Hannah was drunk, and scolded her. Hannah demonstrates that praying is about being earnest and wholehearted when we talk to God.

Look up Daniel chapter 9 verses 4 to 19 to read Daniel's prayer of confession when he is pleading with God to listen to his prayer and act on his plea.

All of Lamentations chapter 5 is a prayer of desperate people who are begging God to relieve them of their suffering.

And, of course, there is the prayer that many people know as the Lord's Prayer, which you can find in Matthew chapter 6 verses 9 to 13. It is the prayer that Jesus used when he taught his disciples how to pray:

"Our Father which art in heaven, Hallowed be thy name.

Thy kingdom come, Thy will be done in earth, as it is in heaven. Give us this day our daily bread. And forgive us our debts, as we forgive our debtors. And lead us not into temptation, but deliver us from evil: For thine is the kingdom, and the power, and the glory, for ever. Amen." (KJV)

However, prayer is not about reading or reciting words from a book; prayer is expressing your personal message to God, your heavenly Father.

Prayer is not for emergencies only. And prayer is not a magic solution to your problems.

Prayer is you talking to God, your heavenly Father, acknowledging his presence, and putting him first in your life.

Prayer is for everyday living as a Christian, walking hand-in-hand with your heavenly Father.

You may want to ask God's support through circumstances that are causing you stress or depression, requesting God's comfort and an answer.

You may want to simply thank God for his goodness and blessings in your life.

Or you may be praying for a loved one who is suffering or dying, asking God for a cure or a peaceful end to their suffering.

I know what you're thinking, and I've been there too.

I know what it's like to feel disappointed by God's response to my prayers.

I have watched many friends and loved ones die, despite our earnest prayers; and it's easy to ask why God is not answering our prayers.

We live in an imperfect world, and bad things happen. Bad things happen because the world in which we live is imperfect. God does not cause illnesses or injuries or injustice, or disabilities or debt or disasters.

I have no doubt that God can cure all problems, but an immediate solution may not be how he answers our prayers. God is not a car breakdown service, and it would be very disrespectful for us to dilute his relationship with us to a formula that we think should work. God will answer our prayers his way.

In my own experience, when my mother was diagnosed with an incurable degenerative illness, although I didn't realize it at the time, God was answering my prayers in a multitude of ways: -

Circumstances aligned to benefit the way in which my mother could be best cared for at home, receiving the most appropriate care when she most needed it.

The most suitable experts became part of my mother's care package when she most needed them.

An opening became available at the most appropriate care facilities at just the right times of need in my mother's regression into residential and nursing care.

Finances became available to adequately cover the costs of my mother's care as expenses mounted.

Time and again, too many things happened in my mother's favor for them all to be explained as coincidence or luck.

And when my mother died, she died comfortably and peacefully in the company of a carer who knew her and loved her.

Prayer may not make bad things go away, but you can know that God is with you every step of the way, and that he is aware of your problems, and that he is caring for you, his way.

If you are a Christian who struggles to pray, if you feel that your prayers are clumsy and childish: relax, because, *'the Spirit helps us in our weakness. We do not know what we ought to pray for, but the Spirit himself intercedes for us through wordless groans. And he who searches our hearts knows the mind of the Spirit, because the Spirit intercedes for God's people in accordance with the will of God.'* (Romans chapter 8 verses 26 and 27 - NIV)

If prayer is new for you, think of God as your Father; speak to God as your loving, caring Father in heaven.
When you pray, you are speaking with a Father who loves you so much that he gave his only Son as a sacrifice so that you could become one of his cherished children.

Praying silently, or praying aloud privately or with a group of friends, however you pray, pray with a whole heart, and God will listen.

'Do not be anxious about anything, but in every situation, by prayer and petition, with thanksgiving, present your requests to God. And the peace of God, which transcends all understanding, will guard your hearts and your minds in Christ Jesus.'
(Philippians, chapter 4 verses 6 and 7 - NIV)

The Resurrection

The resurrection is when Jesus Christ came back to life on the third day after he had been killed by crucifixion.

If Jesus Christ had not come back to life from the dead, at best he could only be called a prophet - just Jesus, not Jesus *Christ*.

If Jesus Christ had not come back to life from the dead, Christianity would not exist.

The resurrection of Jesus Christ is essential to his authenticity.

The resurrection of Jesus Christ proves that there is only one God, only one Savior, and only one hope.

The resurrection of Jesus Christ demonstrates that other religions are without substance.

Jesus declared: *"I am the resurrection and the life. Anyone who believes in me will live, even after dying. Everyone who lives in me and believes in me will never ever die."*
(John chapter 11 verses 25 and 26 - NLT)

What is the importance of the resurrection?

If Jesus Christ had not come back to life from death, there would be no hope for anyone of a life after death.

It would mean that when our body dies: that's it - the end! It would mean that all human life is completely and utterly meaningless.

'Since we preach that Christ rose from the dead, why are some of you saying there will be no resurrection of the dead? For if there is no resurrection of the dead, then Christ has not been raised either.

And if Christ has not been raised, then all our preaching is useless, and your faith is useless. And we apostles would all be lying about God—for we have said that God raised Christ from the grave. But that can't be true if there is no resurrection of the dead.

And if there is no resurrection of the dead, then Christ has not been raised. And if Christ has not been raised, then your faith is useless and you are still guilty of your sins. In that case, all who have died believing in Christ are lost! And if our hope in Christ is only for this life, we are more to be pitied than anyone in the world.

But in fact, Christ has been raised from the dead. He is the first of a great harvest of all who have died.'

(1 Corinthians chapter 15 verses 12 to 20 - NLT)

Resurrection was predicted in the Old Testament

In the Old Testament, Job had suffered a series of personal disasters, and exclaimed: *"Can the dead live again? If so, this would give me hope through all my years of struggle, and I would eagerly await the release of death."*

(Job chapter 14 verse 14 - NLT)

However, despite his suffering Job later declares: *"But as for me, I know that my Redeemer lives, and he will stand upon the earth at last. And after my body has decayed, yet in my body I will see God! I will see him for myself. Yes, I will see him with my own eyes. I am overwhelmed at the thought!' But I know there is someone in heaven who will come at last to my defense. Even after my skin is eaten by disease, while still in this body I will see God.'*

(Job chapter 19 verses 25 to 27 - NLT)

'Those who die in the Lord will live; their bodies will rise again! Those who sleep in the earth will rise up and sing for

joy! For your [God's] *life-giving light will fall like dew on your people in the place of the dead!'*
(Isaiah chapter 26 verse 19 - NLT)

In the Old Testament book of Daniel, a special messenger of God described some of the events of the end of time. *"There will be a time of anguish greater than any since nations first came into existence. But at that time every one of your people whose name is written in the book will be rescued. Many of those whose bodies lie dead and buried will rise up, some to everlasting life and some to shame and everlasting disgrace. Those who are wise will shine as bright as the sky, and those who lead many to righteousness will shine like the stars forever."*
(Daniel chapter 12 verses 1 to 3 - NLT)

However, the resurrection of the dead that is mentioned in the Old Testament was on hold.

Something very special needed to happen before it would be possible for the dead to rise again. The very special event that needed to happen was the sacrifice and resurrection of Jesus Christ.

The sacrifice that Jesus Christ made on the cross has allowed God to forgive our sins. This sacrifice that Jesus Christ made on our behalf, has defeated sin.

Jesus Christ defeated sin.
And Jesus Christ defeated death.

Jesus Christ defeated death when he returned to life on the third day after he had been crucified.

What this means for you is that when you ask God to forgive you, you free yourself from God's condemnation, which means that you can look forward to life after death that will be a wonderful eternal existence in the presence of God.

Jesus Christ assured his disciples that, *"Since I live, you also will live. When I am raised to life again, you will know that I am in my Father, and you are in me, and I am in you."* (John chapter 14 verses 19 and 20 - NLT)

Why does there need to be a resurrection?

'The LORD God placed the man [Adam] *in the Garden of Eden to tend and watch over it. But the LORD God warned him, "You may freely eat the fruit of every tree in the garden— except the tree of the knowledge of good and evil. If you eat its fruit, you are sure to die."* (Genesis chapter 2 verses 15 to 17 - NLT)

You know what happened next: God gave Adam a companion, a wife called Eve; however the serpent deceived Eve and tempted her to take the forbidden fruit, which she shared with Adam.

This is when sin entered the world, and with sin came death: *"If you eat this fruit, you are sure to die."* Death is the inevitable consequence of sin.

However, God has provided the solution to your sins; and by providing the solution to your sins, God has also provided you with the opportunity of eternal life.

When you believe, and ask God to forgive your sins, you are made acceptable to God because Jesus Christ has already made the sacrifice that God needed to forgive all of your sins. This means that when God forgives your sins, you can look forward to eternal life.

'For the wages of sin is death, but the free gift of God is eternal life through Christ Jesus our Lord.' (Romans chapter 6 verse 23 - NLT)

What does the resurrection mean to Christians?

Hope.

The resurrection means that this life of hardships and sorrow and disappointment and pain is not all there is: it means that there is a new and wonderful life to look forward to.

Two criminals were crucified on either side of Jesus Christ; one of the criminals scoffed at Jesus: *"So you're the Messiah, are you? Prove it by saving yourself—and us, too, while you're at it!"* But the other criminal protested, *"Don't you fear God even when you have been sentenced to die? We deserve to die for our crimes, but this man hasn't done anything wrong."* Then he said, *"Jesus, remember me when you come into your Kingdom."* And Jesus replied, *"I assure you, today you will be with me in paradise."*
(Luke chapter 23 verses 39 to 43 - NLT)

Today, you will be with Jesus Christ in paradise.

Paradise!

When a believer dies, their soul enters paradise.

What about non-believers?

Unfortunately, there is no hope for unbelievers.

Jesus said: *"I tell you the truth, those who listen to my message and believe in God who sent me have eternal life. They will never be condemned for their sins, but they have already passed from death into life. And I assure you that the time is coming, indeed it's here now, when the dead will*

171

hear my voice—the voice of the Son of God. And those who listen will live. The Father has life in himself, and he has granted that same life-giving power to his Son. And he has given him authority to judge everyone because he is the Son of Man. Don't be so surprised! Indeed, the time is coming when all the dead in their graves will hear the voice of God's Son, and they will rise again. Those who have done good will rise to experience eternal life, and those who have continued in evil will rise to experience judgment.
(John chapter 5 verses 24 to 29 - NLT)

Unfortunately, the souls of non-believers will be condemned to the Lake of Fire.
(Read the article on Hell for more information about this destiny for unbelievers.)

How will our resurrection happen?

There are two parts to your being:

There is the physical part, your human body;

And there is your soul, which is the person and personality that makes you who you are.

Let me use a vehicular metaphor to explain: -

When I was young I watched my grandmother decline towards her death, and I came to terms with her regression by likening her to a driver in a car.

Her eyes grew dim, as if the car battery could no longer power the headlamps; she gradually became less mobile, as if the tires were flat and the wheel bearings lacked lubrication; her breathing became difficult, as if the carburetor was clogged and the spark plugs weren't firing correctly.

It was just as if the little vehicle in which my granny was driving along through life was finally falling apart.

Then, one afternoon, the engine stopped altogether.

And my granny stepped out of her vehicle.

When my granny died, her soul left her worn-out body.

When we buried my granny, we buried her body.

But her soul had left her body at the moment of her death.

What happens to a believer's soul when they die?

As a believer, when you die, your soul leaves your dead body to be with Jesus Christ in Paradise.

This is confirmed when Jesus Christ stated to the believing criminal who was crucified next to him, *"I assure you, today you will be with me in paradise."*
(Luke chapter 23 verse 43 - NLT)

What happens to a believer's body when they die?

Well, you probably already know: their body is usually put into a big box and buried in a cemetery.

However, that's not the end of the matter.

Paul explains that the bodies of dead believers will be raised to life: *'Our earthly bodies are planted in the ground when we die, but they will be raised to live forever. Our bodies are buried in brokenness, but they will be raised in glory. They are buried in weakness, but they will be raised in strength. They are buried as natural human bodies, but they will be raised as spiritual bodies. For just as there are natural bodies, there are also spiritual bodies.*

The Scriptures tell us, "The first man, Adam, became a living person." But the last Adam—that is, Christ—is a life-giving Spirit. What comes first is the natural body, then the spiritual body comes later. Adam, the first man, was made from the dust of the earth, while Christ, the second man, came from heaven. Earthly people are like the earthly man, and heavenly people are like the heavenly man. Just as we are now like the earthly man, we will someday be like the heavenly man.

What I am saying, dear brothers and sisters, is that our physical bodies cannot inherit the Kingdom of God. These dying bodies cannot inherit what will last forever.'
(1 Corinthians chapter 15 verses 42 to 50 - NLT)

What this means is that when Jesus Christ returns to for the Judgment, the physical body of each dead believer will be raised bodily from the grave to be united with their soul.

'We will not all die, but we will all be transformed! It will happen in a moment, in the blink of an eye, when the last trumpet is blown. For when the trumpet sounds, those who have died will be raised to live forever. And we who are living will also be transformed. For our dying bodies must be transformed into bodies that will never die; our mortal bodies must be transformed into immortal bodies. Then, when our dying bodies have been transformed into bodies that will never die, this Scripture will be fulfilled: "Death is swallowed up in victory. O death, where is your victory? O death, where is your sting?"
(1 Corinthians chapter 15 verses 51 to 55 - NLT)

Paul explained, *'what will happen to the believers who have died so you will not grieve like people who have no hope. For since we believe that Jesus died and was raised to life again, we also believe that when Jesus returns, God will bring back with him the believers who have died. We tell you this directly from the Lord: We who are still living when the Lord returns will not meet him ahead of those who have died. For the Lord himself will come down from heaven with a commanding shout, with the voice of the archangel, and with the trumpet call of God. First, the believers who have died will rise from their graves. Then, together with them, we who are still alive and remain on the earth will be caught up in the clouds to meet the Lord in the air. Then we will be with the Lord forever.'*

(1 Thessalonians chapter 4 verses 13 to 17 - NLT)

If my body will be resurrected from the grave, won't it be decayed?

What if I was killed by a huge explosion and blown to smithereens, how will my body be resurrected if there was nothing left of it?

What if I died with a mental or physical disability, will I be disabled when I am resurrected?

Jesus Christ, *'will take our weak mortal bodies and change them into glorious bodies like his own, using the same power with which he will bring everything under his control.'*
(Philippians chapter 3 verse 21 - NLT)

How's that!

Believers will receive a new and immortal body, which is changed into a glorious body like that of Jesus Christ.

'Some skeptic is sure to ask, "Show me how resurrection works. Give me a diagram; draw me a picture. What does this 'resurrection body' look like?" If you look at this ques-

tion closely, you realize how absurd it is. There are no diagrams for this kind of thing. We do have a parallel experience in gardening. You plant a "dead" seed; soon there is a flourishing plant. There is no visual likeness between seed and plant. You could never guess what a tomato would look like by looking at a tomato seed. What we plant in the soil and what grows out of it don't look anything alike. The dead body that we bury in the ground and the resurrection body that comes from it will be dramatically different. You will notice that the variety of bodies is stunning. Just as there are different kinds of seeds, there are different kinds of bodies—humans, animals, birds, fish—each unprecedented in its form. You get a hint at the diversity of resurrection glory by looking at the diversity of bodies not only on earth but in the skies—sun, moon, stars—all these varieties of beauty and brightness. And we're only looking at pre-resurrection "seeds"—who can imagine what the resurrection "plants" will be like! This image of planting a dead seed and raising a live plant is a mere sketch at best, but perhaps it will help in approaching the mystery of the resurrection body—but only if you keep in mind that when we're raised, we're raised for good, alive forever! The corpse that's planted is no beauty, but when it is raised, it is glorious. Put in the ground weak, it comes up powerful. The seed sown is natural; the seed grown is supernatural—same seed, same body, but what a difference from when it goes down in physical mortality to when it is raised up in spiritual immortality!'

(1 Corinthians chapter 15 verses 35 to 44 - MSG)

In a nutshell: -

When a believer dies: their body is buried, and their soul enters paradise.

Then, when Jesus Christ returns, the bodies of believers will exit their graves and be transformed into glorious spiritual bodies.

When an unbeliever dies: their body is buried, and their soul enters the hopeless emptiness and complete separation from God, which is the underworld.

Then, when Jesus Christ returns, they will face the Judgment, and the souls of unbelievers will be thrown into the Lake of Fire to suffer torment forever and ever.

What were the events surrounding the resurrection of Jesus Christ?

The resurrection of Christ is important to understand and believe, because other religions try very hard to convince people that Jesus was not resurrected. Other religions attempt to discredit the resurrection of Jesus, because the biblical truth of the resurrection of Christ means that their opposing religious belief is proved meaningless.

Jesus Christ was crucified to death.

He had been beaten, he had been flogged with a lead-tipped whip. He had been nailed to a cross, suspended by iron nails that had been hammered through his hands and feet. He had been left hanging in agony for six hours before he died. And then a Roman soldier plunged a spear into Jesus' side to make sure that he was definitely dead.

Jesus was definitely dead.

Jesus had been executed on Friday, which is the day of preparation before the Sabbath [Saturday].

As evening approached, a wealthy man called Joseph appealed to the Roman Governor, Pilate; Joseph asked Pilate for the body of Jesus. Joseph was from Arimathea, and he was an honored member of the Jewish High Council; however, Joseph was also a secret disciple of Christ, (Joseph was secretly a disciple of Christ because he feared the Jewish leaders).

Pilate didn't believe that Jesus was already dead, so he called for a Roman officer to confirm that Jesus was truly dead. Pilate waited for the Roman officer to confirm that Jesus was definitely dead before he allowed Joseph to take his dead body down from the cross.

Joseph, and his colleague Nicodemus, removed Jesus from the cross. Nicodemus had brought about 100 pounds in weight of perfumed ointment made from myrrh and aloes to apply to the body of Jesus as they wrapped him in long sheets of linen cloth.

Joseph owned a new tomb, which had been carved out of the rock in a nearby garden; he laid the body of Jesus in this new tomb. Then Joseph rolled a great stone across the entrance to the tomb to secure it, and left.

Mary Magdalene and Mary the mother of Joseph were sitting across from the tomb, watching.

The next day, the Sabbath, the leading priests and Pharisees went to see Pilate. They insisted that the tomb of Jesus was sealed more securely.

The reason why they wanted the tomb sealed was because Jesus had stated that he would rise from the dead on the third day. However, they suspected that the disciples of Jesus might come and steal his body, and then falsely claim that he had risen from the dead. Pilate agreed to these demands, and ordered for the tomb to be sealed, and for guards to be posted to protect it from any interference.

Early on the Sunday morning, just as the day was dawning, Mary Magdalene and Mary the mother of Joseph went to visit the tomb of Jesus.

Suddenly there was an earthquake. The great stone had rolled away from the entrance of the tomb, and sitting on top of it was an angel wearing clothes as white as snow, whose face shone like lightening.

The Roman guards shook with fear when they saw the angel, and fell into a dead faint.

The angel spoke to the women, saying, *"Don't be afraid!" I know you are looking for Jesus, who was crucified. He isn't here! He is risen from the dead, just as he said would happen. Come, see where his body was lying. And now, go quickly and tell his disciples that he has risen from the dead, and he is going ahead of you to Galilee. You will see him there. Remember what I have told you."*
(Matthew chapter 28 verses 5 to 7 - NLT)

The women were frightened but filled with great joy, and rushed to deliver the angel's message to the disciples. As they were leaving, Jesus met them and greeted them. Jesus said, *"Don't be afraid. Go tell my brothers to leave for Galilee, and they will see me there."* (NLT)

As this was happening, some of the guards had run to the city to tell the leading priests what had happened.

A meeting with the elders was called, and they decided to give the soldiers a large bribe: they paid the soldiers to lie. The religious leaders paid the soldiers to say that the disciples of Jesus came during the night and stole his body while the guards were asleep.

The fact that Jesus had been killed is unquestioned.

Jesus had been killed by the grievous wounds of his punishment and by the agony of crucifixion: his death was confirmed when a soldier plunged a spear deep into the side of Jesus' abdomen.

Jesus had definitely been killed.

And on the third day, just as Jesus had prophesied, he was raised from the dead.

Who are the eyewitnesses to the resurrection?

The first person Jesus physically presented himself to was Mary Magdalene.

Mary had visited the tomb of Jesus early that morning, only to discover it to be empty. Thinking that the body of Jesus had been stolen, she began to weep.

'She turned to leave and saw someone standing there. It was Jesus, but she didn't recognize him. "Dear woman, why are you crying?" Jesus asked her. "Who are you looking for?" She thought he was the gardener. "Sir," she said, "if you have taken him away, tell me where you have put him, and I will go and get him."

"Mary!" Jesus said.

She turned to him and cried out, "Rabboni!" (which is

Hebrew for "Teacher"). (John chapter 20 verses 14 to 16 - NLT)

Jesus physically presented himself to his disciples.

Late in the day on which Jesus Christ had risen from death, *'the disciples were meeting behind locked doors because they were afraid of the Jewish leaders. Suddenly, Jesus was standing there among them! "Peace be with you," he said. As he spoke, he showed them the wounds in his hands and his side. They were filled with joy when they saw the Lord!'* (John chapter 20 verses 19 and 20 - NLT)

The disciple called Thomas had not been present when Jesus appeared to the disciples; Thomas did not believe the others when they told him that Jesus had visited them. Thomas told the other disciples: *"I won't believe it unless I see the nail wounds in his hands, put my fingers into them, and place my hand into the wound in his side." Eight days later the disciples were together again, and this time Thomas was with them. The doors were locked; but suddenly, as before, Jesus was standing among them. "Peace be with you," he said. Then he said to Thomas, "Put your finger here, and look at my hands. Put your hand into the wound in my side. Don't be faithless any longer. Believe!" "My Lord and my God!" Thomas exclaimed. Then Jesus told him, "You believe because you have seen me. Blessed are those who believe without seeing me."*
(John chapter 20 verses 25 to 29 - NLT)

Jesus physically presented himself to two of his followers who were walking to the village of Emmaus, seven miles from Jerusalem.

As the two men walked and talked about everything that had recently happened, Jesus Christ suddenly began walking with them, but God kept them from recognizing Jesus.

Jesus quizzed the two men about what they were discussing, and they sadly explained that the person whom they believed to be their Savior, had been killed.

But Jesus corrected their thinking, quoting from the ancient scriptures about how the Messiah would have to suffer all these things before entering glory.

Nearing the end of their journey to Emmaus, *'Jesus acted as if he were going on, but they begged him, "Stay the night with us, since it is getting late." So he went home with them. As they sat down to eat, he took the bread and blessed it. Then he broke it and gave it to them. Suddenly, their eyes were opened, and they recognized him. And at that moment he disappeared!'*

(Luke chapter 24 verses 28 to 31 - NLT)

Paul briefly lists the people who saw Jesus Christ after his resurrection: *'Christ died for our sins, just as the Scriptures said. He was buried, and he was raised from the dead on the third day, just as the Scriptures said. He was seen by Peter and then by the Twelve. After that, he was seen by more than 500 of his followers at one time, most of whom are still alive, though some have died. Then he was seen by James and later by all the apostles.'*

(1 Corinthians chapter 15 verses 3 to 7 - NLT)

In each of these appearances after his death and resurrection, a couple of important facts are clear: -

Jesus was not displaying any difficulties or disabilities as a result of his brutal punishment. He had been beaten, he had been flogged with a lead-tipped whip, he had been nailed to the cross with large iron nails hammered through his hands and feet, and he had been impaled with a spear.

Yet, despite all of these grievous injuries, Jesus appeared without pain or discomfort: Jesus walked with the two men on the road to Emmaus; Jesus asked Thomas to place his fingers into the holes in his nail-pierced hands, and asked Thomas to place his hand into the spear wound in his side.

The other obvious fact is that these appearances of Jesus, so recently after his death and resurrection, are physical, bodily appearances. Jesus did not appear like a ghost: Jesus appeared in physical form. Thomas even placed his fingers into the nail wounds in his hands, and placed his hand into the spear wound in his side.

'During the forty days after he [Jesus] *suffered and died, he appeared to the apostles from time to time, and he proved to them in many ways that he was actually alive. And he talked to them about the Kingdom of God.'*
(Acts chapter 1 verse 3 - NLT)

The departure of Jesus up to heaven takes place while he is with his apostles: *'they gathered around him and asked him, "Lord, are you at this time going to restore the kingdom to Israel?" He said to them: "It is not for you to know the times or dates the Father has set by his own authority. But you will receive power when the Holy Spirit comes on you; and you will be my witnesses in Jerusalem, and in all Judea and Samaria, and to the ends of the earth." After he said this, he was taken up before their very eyes, and a cloud hid him from their sight. They were looking intently up into the sky as he was going, when suddenly two men dressed in white stood beside them. "Men of Galilee," they said, "why do you stand here looking into the sky? This same Jesus, who has been taken from you into heaven, will come back in the same way you have seen him go into heaven."* (Acts chapter 1 verses 6 to 11 - NIV)

After his ascent to heaven, does Jesus Christ appear again?

Jesus appeared to Paul as he was approaching Damascus. Paul was enveloped in a bright light, and a voice asked, *"Why are you persecuting me?"* Paul (who was at that time called Saul) asked who was speaking: *'the voice replied, "I am Jesus, the one you are persecuting!"* (Acts chapter 9 verse 5 - NLT)

Jesus appeared to Stephen as he is being condemned to death for his faith in Christ: *'But Stephen, full of the Holy Spirit, gazed steadily into heaven and saw the glory of God, and he saw Jesus standing in the place of honor at God's right hand.'* (Acts chapter 7 verse 55 - NLT)

And Jesus Christ, the Son of God is revealed to John in the book of Revelation. John described someone, *'like the Son of Man'* who said to John, *"Don't be afraid! I am the First and the Last. I am the living one. I died, but look—I am alive forever and ever! And I hold the keys of death and the grave."* (Revelation chapter 1 verses 17 and 18 - NLT)

Where is Jesus Christ now?

Jesus Christ is in heaven.
'Because of the joy awaiting him, he endured the cross,

disregarding its shame. Now he is seated in the place of honor beside God's throne.'
(Hebrews chapter 12 verse 2 - NLT)

Is Jesus Christ coming back?

Yes.

Jesus Christ has told us that he will return.

Jesus Christ will return for the Judgment.

"At last, the sign that the Son of Man is coming will appear in the heavens, and there will be deep mourning among all the peoples of the earth. And they will see the Son of Man coming on the clouds of heaven with power and great glory. And he will send out his angels with the mighty blast of a trumpet, and they will gather his chosen ones from all over the world—from the farthest ends of the earth and heaven."
(Matthew chapter 24 verses 30 and 31 - NLT)

Are you ready for the return of Jesus Christ?

Salvation

The dictionary definition for the word *Salvation* is: *being preserved from harm*.

On most computer programs there is a **Save** option that you need to use when you want to protect your completed work on your computer.

Perhaps you have spent hours working on something, but have neglected to save it: if your computer crashes, or the program stops responding, or if there's a power failure and everything goes blank, what happens?

You know what happens:

All your work is lost.

It is gone.

All your hard work is lost forever, irretrievable, without hope of rescue.

Similarly, if you neglect the option of being saved by God, when you die, your soul will be gone forever, irretrievable, without hope of rescue.

Tapping the **Save** button on your computer program is very simple.

And asking God to save you is also very simple.

Perhaps you don't think that you are important.

Maybe, in this world that idolizes wealthy and successful people, you are a nobody; maybe you are not wealthy, maybe you are not beautiful, maybe you didn't achieve good results at school; maybe you don't have any true friends.

Maybe you are in trouble with debt, or have an addiction to drugs, or alcohol, or gambling, or pornography. Maybe you are the kind of person you really don't want to be.

Maybe you have achieved success and financial security, but realize that your life is empty and meaningless.

Maybe you feel worthless, unloved, unappreciated; maybe you feel hopeless.

Believe this biblical truth: **God loves you**.

How much does God love you?

'This is love: not that we loved God, but that he loved us and sent his Son as an atoning sacrifice for our sins.'
(1 John chapter 4 verse 10 - NIV)

'God demonstrates his own love for us in this: While we were still sinners, Christ died for us.'
(Romans chapter 5 verse 8 - NIV)

God loves you, and he values you so much that he has made it possible for you to become one of his precious children.

However, there's an obstacle: you and I, we are sinners.

Imagine that you've carelessly built up a serous debt that you simply can't repay, not in a million years.

So, you are taken to court, and the judge rules that all of your money and all of your possessions will be taken away, and you will be left completely destitute, penniless, without a hope in the world.

But then a stranger steps forward and pays all your debts, all of your loans, your mortgage, your bank overdraft, and even your credit card balance - everything, every penny: cleared. You are saved from ruin.

How amazing would that be?

Similarly, imagine standing before God to be judged. He would find you unworthy; he would find you to be a worthless sinner.

But just as you are about to be condemned, Jesus Christ steps forward and tells God that it's all right, because he has already accepted the blame and punishment for all of your sins: all your sins are erased and you are saved from condemnation.

Jesus said: *"Everyone who acknowledges me publicly here on earth, I will also acknowledge before my Father in heaven."*

However: *"Everyone who denies me here on earth, I will also deny before my Father in heaven."*
(Matthew chapter 10 verses 32 and 33 - NLT)

Regardless of your lack of money
Regardless of your background
Regardless of your color, or gender, or nationality
Regardless of how many times you have been in trouble or disgraced yourself:
God loves you.

God loves you so much that he has provided you with the opportunity of forgiveness for all of your sins when you accept Jesus Christ as your Savior.

What do you need to do to receive forgiveness?
Exam? *No.*
Application Form? *No.*
Interview? *No.*
Just ask? **YES**!

When you approach God with a sincere heart; when you realize that you are unworthy before God; when you know that your sins are a barrier between you and God: simply ask God to forgive you: and God will forgive you.

'If you declare with your mouth, "Jesus is Lord," and believe in your heart that God raised him from the dead, you will be saved. For it is with your heart that you believe and are justified, and it is with your mouth that you profess your faith and are saved.'
(Romans chapter 10 verse 10 and 11 - NIV)

I was 10 years old when I realized what a horrible person I was becoming; in a moment of deep shame I stopped in my tracks and spoke six words in earnest prayer. I said, "God I'm ashamed. Please forgive me."

God forgave me right there and then. I know he did, because something supernatural immediately happened to me: the Holy Spirit enveloped me with God's love, and has lived in my heart ever since.

God's forgiveness was the most amazing experience I have ever known, and I remember it as clearly as if it were yesterday. Ever since that day, through ups and downs, through my temptations and failures, God has been with me every step of the way.

God adopted me: he is my Father.

God is a Father who will never, ever abandon me.

I am not perfect.

I am a sinner who deserves condemnation; however, *"he* [Jesus] *saved us, not because of righteous things we had done, but because of his mercy."*
(Titus chapter 3 verse 5 - NIV)

We cannot earn salvation by our own efforts: we are only saved because of the love that Jesus Christ poured out for us when he died on the cross.

'In him [Jesus Christ] *we have redemption through his blood, the forgiveness of sins, in accordance with the riches of God's grace that he lavished on us.'*
(Ephesians chapter 1 verse 7 - NIV)

"God so loved the world that he gave his one and only Son, that whoever believes in him shall not perish but have eternal life. Because God did not send his Son into the world to condemn the world, but to save the world through him. Whoever believes in him is not condemned, but who-ever does not believe stands condemned already because they have not believed in the name of God's one and only Son."   (John chapter 3 verses 16 to 18 - NIV)

You do not earn salvation - because Jesus Christ earned it for you when he died on the cross. Salvation is a gift that is freely offered to you by God.
All you need to do is ask.

"Ask and it will be given to you; seek and you will find; knock and the door will be opened to you. For everyone who asks receives; the one who seeks finds; and to the one who knocks, the door will be opened."
(Matthew chapter 7 verses 7 and 8 - NIV)

Salvation is yours as simply as believing and asking.

Satan, the Devil

Do not be misled by the idea that Satan is the equal-opposite to God.

Satan would love us to consider him to be the equal-opposite to God.

Satan is a fallen servant of God.

Satan will never equal God's power and authority.

And God will destroy Satan.

In the Garden of Eden, the serpent deceived Eve.

'The serpent was more crafty than any other beast of the field that the Lord God had made'
(Genesis chapter 3 verse 1 - NLT)

God had given a strict warning to Adam that he must not eat the fruit from the Tree of the Knowledge of Good and Evil, which was in the middle of the Garden of Eden. God had told Adam, *"if you eat its fruit, you are sure to die."* (Genesis chapter 2 verse 17 - NLT)

However, the serpent deceived Eve: *"You won't die!" the serpent replied to the woman. "God knows that your eyes will be opened as soon as you eat it, and you will be like God, knowing both good and evil." The woman was convinced. She saw that the tree was beautiful and its fruit looked delicious, and she wanted the wisdom it would give her. So she took some of the fruit and ate it. Then she gave some to her husband, who was with her, and he ate it, too.'*
(Genesis chapter 3 verse 4 - NLT)

This is when it all went wrong.

This is when and where and how sin entered the world.

Things were wonderful, until the serpent deceived Eve.

Who was that serpent?

John identifies this serpent for us in the book of Revelation: *'that ancient serpent, who is called the devil and Satan, the deceiver of the whole world—he was thrown down to the earth, and his angels were thrown down with him.'* (Revelation chapter 12 verse 9 - ESV)

Where did Satan come from?

In the book of Ezekiel, God sent a message to the king of Tyre, who was an evil king benefiting from the power given to him by Satan. God addressed this message directly at Satan: *'You had everything going for you. You were in Eden, God's garden. You were dressed in splendor, your robe studded with jewels: carnelian, peridot, and moonstone, beryl, onyx, and jasper, sapphire, turquoise, and emerald, all in settings of engraved gold. A robe was prepared for you the same day you were created. You were the anointed cherub. I placed you on the mountain of God. You strolled in magnificence among the stones of fire. From the day of your creation you were sheer perfection,... and then imperfection—evil!—was detected in you. In much buying and selling you turned violent, you sinned! I threw you, disgraced, off the mountain of God. I threw you out—you, the anointed angel-cherub. No more strolling among the gems of fire for you! Your beauty went to your head. You corrupted wisdom by using it to get worldly fame.'*
(Ezekiel chapter 28 verses 12 to 17 - MSG)

Did you notice here that Satan is twice identified as not just a cherub, but as an *anointed cherub*: this is an important high-ranking cherub.

Satan is an anointed cherub who rebelled against God, and was expelled from heaven.

What is a cherub?

The plural of cherub is, cherubim. Cherubim are mighty and powerful guardians of God, and are depicted guarding the heavenly throne of God: *'The Lord reigns, let nations tremble; he sits enthroned between the cherubim, let the earth shake.'* (Psalm 99 verse 1 - NIV)

Cherubim are described by Ezekiel: *'From the center of the cloud came four living beings that looked human, except that each had four faces and four wings.*

Their legs were straight, and their feet had hooves like those of a calf and shone like burnished bronze. Under each of their four wings I could see human hands. So each of the four beings had four faces and four wings. The wings of each living being touched the wings of the beings beside it. Each one moved straight forward in any direction without turning around.

Each had a human face in the front, the face of a lion on the right side, the face of an ox on the left side, and the face of an eagle at the back.

Each had two pairs of outstretched wings—one pair stretched out to touch the wings of the living beings on either side of it, and the other pair covered its body. They went in whatever direction the spirit chose, and they moved straight forward in any direction without turning around. The living beings looked like bright coals of fire or brilliant torches, and lightning seemed to flash back and forth among them. And the living beings darted to and fro like flashes of lightning.' (Ezekiel chapter 1 verses 5 to 13 - NLT)

What does Satan look like?

You're probably thinking to yourself: if Satan is a cherub with four wings and four different faces, he is going to be easy to recognize in a crowd.

However, Satan is a spiritual being.

In the book of Genesis, Satan is the serpent who deceived Eve, misleading her into eating the fruit of the Tree of the Knowledge of Good and Evil.

Because of this evil deception, God told the serpent, *"I will put enmity between you and the woman, and between your offspring and hers; he will crush your head, and you will strike his heel."* (Genesis chapter 3 verse 15 - NIV)

Here, God is addressing Satan, telling him that the day will come when Jesus Christ will undo the damage that Satan's deception has caused.

In the book of Isaiah, God's sends a message taunting the king of Babylon: *'How you are fallen from heaven, O shining star, son of the morning! You have been thrown down to the earth, you who destroyed the nations of the world. For you said to yourself, 'I will ascend to heaven and set my throne above God's stars. I will preside on the mountain of the gods far away in the north. I will climb to the highest heavens and be like the Most High.' Instead, you will be brought down to the place of the dead, down to its lowest depths."* (Isaiah chapter 14 verses 12 to 15 - NLT)

Here, God's message was to the king of Babylon; however, God is directly addressing Satan who has been empowering the king of Babylon.

At the last supper with his disciples, Jesus knew that

his friend Judas was going to betray him to the chief priest, which would inevitably lead to a horrible death on the cross. Jesus passed the bread to Judas. *'When Judas had eaten the bread, Satan entered into him. Then Jesus told him, "Hurry and do what you're going to do." None of the others at the table knew what Jesus meant.'* (John chapter 13 verses 27 and 28 - NLT)

Jesus knew that Satan had entered the heart of Judas, and it was Satan who caused him to betray Jesus.

Satan was controlling the serpent.

Satan was controlling the king of Tyre.

Satan was controlling the king of Babylon.

And Judas Iscariot was under the power of Satan.

As a spiritual being, Satan does not go about the earth in the form of a cherub. Satan's evil spirit enters the hearts of men and animals, and he makes them his instruments of evil.

Where is Satan?

Satan is right here,

On earth,

Right now.

'War arose in heaven, Michael and his angels fighting against the dragon [Satan]. And the dragon and his angels fought back, but he was defeated, and there was no longer any place for them in heaven. And the great dragon was thrown down, that ancient serpent, who is called the devil and Satan, the deceiver of the whole world—he was thrown down to the earth, and his angels were thrown down with him.' (Revelation chapter 12 verses 7 to 9 - ESV)

Satan and his angels inhabit the earth, which explains

why there is so much wickedness, injustice and suffering in the world.

In the book of Job, *'The LORD said to Satan, "From where have you come?" Satan answered the LORD and said, "From going to and fro on the earth, and from walking up and down on it."* (Job chapter 1 verse 7 - ESV)

Watch out!

Please, watch out.

Satan is wandering about the earth, seeking opportunities to cause trouble and lead us into evil.

'Be alert and of sober mind. Your enemy the devil prowls around like a roaring lion looking for someone to devour.'
(1 Peter chapter 5 verse 8 - NIV)

What does Satan do?

In the book of Revelation, John calls Satan, *'the deceiver of the whole world.'* (Revelation chapter 12 verse 9 - ESV)

Just as Satan deceived Eve, and brought sin into the world, Satan is still deceiving and corrupting people today. Satan is wandering the earth, seeking opportunities to affect and infect people with evil.

Satan actively deceives and corrupts people.

In the Gospel of Matthew chapter 4 verses 1 to 11, Satan even attempts to test and deceive Jesus Christ; but Jesus knew what Satan was trying to do; Jesus resisted temptation, and rebuked Satan.

Satan leads people to accept things that are totally unacceptable to God.

Many sins have been normalized in our world today.

Many sins have even become socially acceptable.

Some sinful practices that are despicable to God are openly promoted in the media.

Some sinful practices that are despicable to God are even protected under government legislation.

'When you follow the desires of your sinful nature, the results are very clear: sexual immorality, impurity, lustful pleasures, idolatry, sorcery, hostility, quarreling, jealousy, outbursts of anger, selfish ambition, dissension, division, envy, drunkenness, wild parties, and other sins like these. Let me tell you again, as I have before, that anyone living that sort of life will not inherit the Kingdom of God.'
(Galatians chapter 5 verses 19 to 21 - NLT)

Why does Satan want to deceive people?

God loves you.

Even though you and I are sinners, God loves us.

God wants everyone to believe in the salvation bought for us by the sacrifice Jesus Christ made on the cross.

But Satan is deceiving people and stealing them away from God.

Satan is deceiving and corrupting people everywhere.

Satan deceives and corrupts ordinary people like you and me.

Satan deceives and corrupts people in authority.

Satan deceives and corrupts powerful people like kings and presidents, and he makes them his servants.

Satan can infect the hearts of Christians, and lead them into temptation and destroy their lives and relationships and reputation.

Even a respectable person who appears wholesome and trustworthy may be a servant of Satan.

Paul warns that the profiteers who are making themselves wealthy by preaching the message of the New Testament, are servants of Satan: *'These people are false apostles. They are deceitful workers who disguise themselves as apostles of Christ. But I am not surprised! Even Satan disguises himself as an angel of light. So it is no wonder that his servants also disguise themselves as servants of righteousness. In the end they will get the punishment their wicked deeds deserve.'*
(2 Corinthians chapter 11 verses 13 to 15 - NLT)

Satan is the god of this world

Because Satan is the god of this world, people are being led away from God in large numbers; people are being deceived into believing that God does not exist. And because popular opinion has such a powerful influence, once an idea is accepted in the media, multitudes of people willingly follow that wrong way of thinking.

People instinctively follow the crowd, even when the crowd is in the fast lane on the highway to hell.

"You can enter God's Kingdom only through the narrow gate. The highway to hell is broad, and its gate is wide for the many who choose that way. But the gateway to life is very narrow and the road is difficult, and only a few ever find it." (Matthew chapter 7 verses 13 and 14 - NLT)

Satan deceives people, and he is very effective at convincing them that God does not exist. Satan blinds the minds of people who do not believe in God.

And the terrible truth is that people don't realize that Satan is influencing and corrupting them.

'Satan, who is the god of this world, has blinded the minds of those who don't believe. They are unable to see the glorious light of the Good News. They don't understand this message about the glory of Christ, who is the exact likeness of God.' (2 Corinthians chapter 4 verse 4 - NLT)

What is God going to do with Satan?

The end has already been decided for Satan.

In the book of Revelation, Jesus Christ reveals Satan's fate to John: 'The devil, who had deceived them, was thrown into the fiery lake of burning sulfur, joining the beast and the false prophet. There they will be tormented day and night forever and ever.'
(Revelation chapter 20 verse 10 - NLT)

What about all the people who have been deceived by Satan?

"Just as the weeds are sorted out and burned in the fire, so it will be at the end of the world. The Son of Man will send his angels, and they will remove from his Kingdom everything that causes sin and all who do evil. And the angels will throw them into the fiery furnace, where there will be weeping and gnashing of teeth.

Then the righteous will shine like the sun in their Father's Kingdom. Anyone with ears to hear should listen and understand!" (Matthew chapter 13 verses 40 to 43 - NLT)

What can we do to protect ourselves from Satan?

When Jesus taught his disciples how they should pray, he told them that they should ask for protection from Satan: "And lead us not into temptation, but deliver us from the evil one." (Matthew chapter 6 verse 13 - NIV)

When we pray, Jesus advised that we should ask God to help us to resist the temptations of Satan.

Remember that when you accept Jesus Christ as your Savior, you become a child of God.

God adopts you as one of his children.

When Satan succeeds in tempting one of God's children into sin, Satan knows that this will hurt God.

Any parent who has lost a child will tell you how painful it is. And it hurts God when his children are lost.

Satan is not powerful enough to hurt God directly; so instead, Satan hurts the people whom God loves: Satan hurts God's children, knowing that hurting God's children is hurting God.

'Be strong in the Lord and in the strength of his might. Put on the whole armor of God, that you may be able to stand against the schemes of the devil. For we do not wrestle against flesh and blood, but against the rulers, against the authorities, against the cosmic powers over this present darkness, against the spiritual forces of evil in the heavenly places. Therefore take up the whole armor of God, that you may be able to withstand in the evil day, and having done all, to stand firm.'
(Ephesians chapter 6 verses 10 to 13 - ESV)

The Son of God
Jesus Christ, the Messiah

Let me start by explaining the name: Jesus Christ.
Jesus is the Greek form of the Hebrew name *Joshua*.
The name Jesus [and Joshua] means: God Saves.

Christ is not the surname of Jesus: Christ is his title.
The word *Christ* comes from the Greek word *Christos*,
which can be translated as *the anointed one,* or, *the
chosen one*.

Jesus is also referred to as the *Messiah*.
The word *Messiah* is the Hebrew equivalent of the word
Christ - same title, just a different language.
The Bible refers to Jesus as both Messiah and Christ
because the Old Testament was originally written in the
Hebrew language, and the New Testament was origi-
nally written in the Greek language.

Who is Jesus Christ?

There is one God: God the Father, God the Son, and
God the Holy Spirit.
God is a spiritual being, he is not made of flesh and
blood like we are, which meant that when God sent his
Son to live among us, the Son of God had to take on
human form.
Jesus Christ is the Son of God in human form.
Jesus Christ stated: *"I and my Father are one."*
(John chapter 10 verse 30 - KJV)

About 1,500 years ago when Patrick was converting the

people of Ireland to Christianity, his listeners demanded a clearer explanation of how God can be three beings, and how three beings can be one God.

Patrick plucked a little shamrock leaf that was growing at his feet, and held it up for all to see.

The shamrock has a leaf with three distinct sections; Patrick asked his listeners to tell him if the shamrock had one leaf or three.

The people replied that it is both one leaf *and* three.

"And so it is with God," replied Patrick.

Don't feel foolish if you struggle to understand the concept of God existing as the Father, the Son, and the Holy Spirit: Jesus had to explain this same truth to Philip, who was one of the apostles appointed by Jesus.

'Philip said, "Lord, show us the Father, and we will be satisfied." Jesus replied, "Have I been with you all this time, Philip, and yet you still don't know who I am? Anyone who has seen me has seen the Father! So why are you asking me to show him to you? Don't you believe that I am in the Father and the Father is in me? The words I speak are not my own, but my Father who lives in me does his work through me. Just believe that I am in the Father and the Father is in me. Or at least believe because of the work you have seen me do.

(John chapter 14 verses 9 to 11 - NLT)

Does the Son of God feature in the Old Testament?

If God exists as God the Father, the Son, and the Holy Spirit, by applying simple logic, God the Son did not

begin his life as the little baby Jesus born in Bethlehem - God the Son must have also existed forever. And this is confirmed when Jesus Christ reveals himself to John in the book of Revelation, stating: *"I am A to Z. I am The God Who Is, The God Who Was, and The God About to Arrive. I am the Sovereign-Strong."*
(Revelation chapter 1 verse 8 - MSG)

In the opening verses of the Gospel of John, John refers to Jesus Christ as the Word, and writes: *'In the beginning was the Word, and the Word was with God, and the Word was God. He was with God in the beginning. Through him all things were made; without him nothing was made that has been made.'*
(John chapter 1 verses 1 to 3 - NIV)

John is very clear about this: the Son of God, the person known to him as Jesus Christ, existed at the very beginning; furthermore, the Son of God was a primary instrument of God's creation.

Jesus said: *"Truly, truly, I say to you, before Abraham was, I am."* (John chapter 8 verse 58 - ESV) Abraham lived about 1,900 years before the birth of Jesus. And *"I am"* is an odd use of grammar, until you remember the time when God instructed Moses to deliver a personal message to the Israelites: Moses asked God what he should say if the Israelites ask who the message was from. God replied, *"I AM Who I AM." And he said, "Say to the people of Israel: "I AM has sent me to you."*
(Exodus chapter 3 verse 14 - ESV)

The Son of God existed forever before his birth in human form as Jesus; therefore it is logical to suppose that the Son of God may have featured occasionally in the Old Testament.

Where in the Old Testament might the Son of God have featured anonymously?

There appear to be several occasions in the Old Testament where people may possibly have had a personal encounter with the Son of God.

God told Moses that, *"you cannot see my face, for man shall not see me and live."*   (Exodus chapter 33 verse 20 - ESV)

And in the Gospel of John, Jesus states that: *"the Father who sent me has testified about me himself. You have never heard his voice or seen him face to face."*
(John chapter 5 verse 37 - NLT)

If no one can see God's face or hear God's voice, perhaps when people had these personal encounters they were having a personal encounter with the Son of God.

Adam and Eve were hiding from God in the Garden of Eden: *'Then the man and his wife heard the sound of the Lord God as he was walking in the garden in the cool of the day, and they hid from the Lord God among the trees of the garden. But the Lord God called to the man, "Where are you?"*   (Genesis chapter 3 verses 8 and 9 - NIV)

If no one has ever heard the voice of God, is it possible that the person who was searching for Adam and Eve could have been the Son of God?

Jacob wrestled with a man during the night. Grappling furiously together, the man touched Jacob's hip and wrenched it out of its socket.

"What is your name?" the man asked. He replied, "Jacob."

"Your name will no longer be Jacob," the man told him. *"From now on you will be called Israel, because you have fought with God and with men and have won."*
(Genesis chapter 32 verses 24 to 28 - NLT)

Is it possible that the person who wrestled with Jacob was the Son of God?

Joshua faced the daunting task of defeating the city of Jericho: *'When Joshua was near the town of Jericho, he looked up and saw a man standing in front of him with sword in hand. Joshua went up to him and demanded, "Are you friend or foe?" "Neither one," he replied. "I am the commander of the LORD's army." At this, Joshua fell with his face to the ground in reverence. "I am at your command," Joshua said. "What do you want your servant to do?" The commander of the LORD's army replied, "Take off your sandals, for the place where you are standing is holy." And Joshua did as he was told.'*
(Joshua chapter 5 verses 13 to 15 - NLT)

Is it possible that this commander of the LORD's army could have been the Son of God? Why else would the ground have been holy?

Manoah's childless wife was confronted by the angel of the LORD, who told her that she would become pregnant and give birth to a son, Samson.

When the angel of the LORD appeared a second time, Manoah asked the angel to give his name: *"Why do you ask my name?" the angel of the LORD replied. "It is too wonderful for you to understand."*

'Manoah took a young goat and a grain offering and offered it on a rock as a sacrifice to the LORD. And as Manoah and

his wife watched, the LORD did an amazing thing. As the flames from the altar shot up toward the sky, the angel of the LORD ascended in the fire. When Manoah and his wife saw this, they fell with their faces to the ground. The angel did not appear again to Manoah and his wife. Manoah finally realized it was the angel of the LORD, and he said to his wife, "We will certainly die, for we have seen God!" (Judges chapter 13 verses 18 to 21 - NLT)

Is it possible that this angel of the LORD, whose name is too wonderful to understand, is the Son of God?

King Nebuchadnezzar threw Daniel's three companions into the roaring hot flames of the fiery furnace. *'But suddenly, Nebuchadnezzar jumped up in amazement and exclaimed to his advisers, "Didn't we tie up three men and throw them into the furnace?" "Yes, Your Majesty, we certainly did," they replied. "Look!" Nebuchadnezzar shouted. "I see four men, unbound, walking around in the fire unharmed! And the fourth looks like a god!" Then Nebuchadnezzar came as close as he could to the door of the flaming furnace and shouted: "Shadrach, Meshach, and Abednego, servants of the Most High God, come out! Come here!" So Shadrach, Meshach, and Abednego stepped out of the fire. Then the high officers, officials, governors, and advisers crowded around them and saw that the fire had not touched them. Not a hair on their heads was singed, and their clothing was not scorched. They didn't even smell of smoke!'* (Daniel chapter 3 verses 24 to 27 - NLT)

Is it possible that the fourth person, who looked like a god, was actually the Son of God?

The Son of God has always existed. And it is possible

that the Son of God represented God the Father in some of the Old Testament descriptions.

Why did the Son of God need to live among us?

'So the Word became human and made his home among us. He was full of unfailing love and faithfulness. And we have seen his glory, the glory of the Father's one and only Son.'
(John chapter 1 verse 14 - NIV)

Why would the powerful Son of God humble himself to such extremes and live in this world as one of us?

God had planned to send his Son to save the world as long ago as the time of Adam and Eve in the Garden of Eden.

Eve had been deceived and tempted into sin by the serpent, and God told the serpent: *"I will put enmity between you and the woman, and between your offspring and hers; he will crush your head, and you will strike his heel."* (Genesis chapter 3 verse 15 - NIV) The offspring of the woman whom God is referring to, is Jesus Christ.

In the book of Genesis, God told Abraham that, *"All the families on earth will be blessed through you."*
(Genesis chapter 12 verse 3 - NLT)

At the start of the Gospel of Matthew you can read the lineage of Abraham, which ends with Joseph, who adopted Jesus as his own son. That descendant of Abraham who was sent to bless all the families on earth is, Jesus Christ.

God told David, *"When you die and are buried with your ancestors, I will raise up one of your descendants, your own offspring, and I will make his kingdom strong. He is the one who will build a house—a temple—for my name. And I will secure his royal throne forever. I will be his father, and he will be my son."* (2 Samuel chapter 7 verses 12 to 14 - NLT)

Again, look at the lineage described at the start of the Gospel of Matthew, and see how David is a direct ancestor to Joseph, the father of Jesus. The descendant, whom God is telling David about, is Jesus Christ.

Skipping forward about 1,900 years since the time of Abraham, and about 1,000 years since the time of King David, God sent the angel Gabriel to speak with Mary. Gabriel said, *"Do not be afraid, Mary; you have found favor with God. You will conceive and give birth to a son, and you are to call him Jesus. He will be great and will be called the Son of the Most High. The Lord God will give him the throne of his father David, and he will reign over Jacob's descendants forever; his kingdom will never end."*
(Luke chapter 1 verses 30 to 33 - NIV)

Clearly, the child whom Mary conceived by the Holy Spirit is Jesus Christ, the Son of God.

Why did the Son of God arrive in human form?

The Son of God lived among us in human form because God needed the perfect sacrifice that would compensate him for the sins of the world, and allow for the forgiveness of our sins; the only sacrifice that was perfect was his only Son. However, his only Son is a spiritual being, like God, and it would not have been possible to sacrifice a spiritual being.

The Son of God came to live among us as a human, and this allowed him to serve his purpose as the perfect sacrifice when he would be executed by crucifixion.

The Son of God left his heavenly home, and came to earth in human form as the person, Jesus Christ; he did this so that, through his sacrifice, you and I can receive God's forgiveness of our sins.

"For God so loved the world that he gave his one and only Son, that whoever believes in him shall not perish but have eternal life. For God did not send his Son into the world to condemn the world, but to save the world through him." (John chapter 3 verses 16 and 17 - NIV)

How did the sacrifice of Jesus Christ, the Son of God, create the opportunity for our salvation?

In the Old Testament you can read how people offered sacrifices of cattle and sheep and goats to compensate for their sins. For example, God commanded the chief priests to sacrifice a bull every day so that the people could be kept right with God: *"Each day you must sacrifice a young bull as a sin offering to purify them, making them right with the LORD."* (Exodus chapter 29 verse 36 - NLT)

However, the sacrifice that God required to allow him to forgive the sins of the whole world had to be much more special than prize livestock. How could the sacrifice of an animal compensate for the sins of people?

The only sacrifice special enough and perfect enough and important enough to allow God to forgive the sins of everyone, was his only Son.

Jesus told his followers that he came, *"to give his life as a ransom for many."* (Matthew chapter 20 verse 28 - NIV)

This was why the Son of God came to earth as a human.

Jesus Christ knew that he was the sacrifice.

Shortly before he was arrested, Jesus looked up to heaven and prayed: *"Father, the hour has come. Glorify your Son so he can give glory back to you. For you have given him authority over everyone. He gives eternal life to each one you have given him. And this is the way to have eternal life—to know you, the only true God, and Jesus Christ, the one you sent to earth. I brought glory to you here on earth by completing the work you gave me to do. Now, Father, bring me into the glory we shared before the world began."* (John chapter 17 verses 1 to 5 - NLT)

Moments before his arrest, Jesus knew that the time of his great suffering and death was imminent: *"Abba, Father,"* he cried out, *"everything is possible for you. Please take this cup of suffering away from me. Yet I want your will to be done, not mine."* (Mark chapter 14 verse 36 - NLT)

Jesus Christ knew that he had to be killed as the sacrifice that God required to forgive our sins.

Jesus did not attempt to defend himself against the accusations of the priests who wanted to kill him.

700 years before the execution of Jesus, the prophet Isaiah had predicted the sacrifice of the Son of God: *'He was beaten, he was tortured, but he didn't say a word. Like a lamb taken to be slaughtered and like a sheep being sheared, he took it all in silence. Justice miscarried, and he was led off—and did anyone really know what was happening? He died without a thought for his own welfare, beaten bloody for the sins of my people. They buried him with the wicked, threw him in a grave with a rich man, even though he'd never hurt a soul or said one word that wasn't true.'* (Isaiah chapter 53 verses 7 to 9 - MSG)

After he had been arrested, Jesus was dragged in front of the most powerful man in the land, the Roman Governor, Pilate. Pilate had the legal power and authority to free Jesus, or to have him executed. But Jesus made no attempt to defend himself against the accusations of the crowd.

'Again Pilate asked him, "Aren't you going to answer? See how many things they are accusing you of." But Jesus still made no reply, and Pilate was amazed.'

(Mark chapter 15 verses 3 and 4 - NIV)

Pilate authorized the execution of Jesus Christ - death by crucifixion.

And by his death, Jesus Christ became the sacrifice that God needed to forgive our sins.

Jesus Christ defeated death

On the third day after his execution, Jesus Christ was raised from the dead.

Jesus Christ defeated death.

Paul explained what the death and resurrection of Jesus Christ means to believers: -

'Since we have died to sin, how can we continue to live in it? Or have you forgotten that when we were joined with Christ Jesus in baptism, we joined him in his death? For we died and were buried with Christ by baptism. And just as Christ was raised from the dead by the glorious power of the Father, now we also may live new lives. Since we have been united with him in his death, we will also be raised to life as he was. We know that our old sinful selves were crucified with Christ so that sin might lose its power in our lives. We are no longer slaves to sin. For when we died with Christ

213

we were set free from the power of sin. And since we died with Christ, we know we will also live with him. We are sure of this because Christ was raised from the dead, and he will never die again. Death no longer has any power over him. When he died, he died once to break the power of sin. But now that he lives, he lives for the glory of God. So you also should consider yourselves to be dead to the power of sin and alive to God through Christ Jesus.'
(Romans chapter 6 verses 2 to 11 - NLT)

It is the truth that Jesus Christ is the human form of the Son of God.

And as promised by God from the time of Adam and Eve, and from the time of Abraham, and from the time of David, (and also prophesied many, many times throughout the Old Testament), Jesus Christ was the sacrifice that God required that allowed him to offer the forgiveness of sins for everyone.

Jesus Christ is the Savior.

Jesus Christ is your Savior.

'Even before he made the world, God loved us and chose us in Christ to be holy and without fault in his eyes. God decided in advance to adopt us into his own family by bringing us to himself through Jesus Christ. This is what he wanted to do, and it gave him great pleasure.

So we praise God for the glorious grace he has poured out on us who belong to his dear Son. He is so rich in kindness and grace that he purchased our freedom with the blood of his Son and forgave our sins.'
(Ephesians chapter 1 verses 4 to 7 - NLT)

The Son of God is coming back

Throughout the Old Testament, the return of Christ is predicted and promised.

The birth of Jesus Christ was promised by God and prophesied hundreds of times: and this has already taken place.

The *return* of Jesus Christ is predicted thousands of times throughout the Bible: Jesus Christ will return for the Judgment.

"And then at last, the sign that the Son of Man is coming will appear in the heavens, and there will be deep mourning among all the peoples of the earth. And they will see the Son of Man coming on the clouds of heaven with power and great glory. And he will send out his angels with the mighty blast of a trumpet, and they will gather his chosen ones from all over the world—from the farthest ends of the earth and heaven." (Matthew chapter 24 verses 30 and 31 - NLT)

Jesus Christ is our Savior: he was the sacrifice that has allowed God to forgive your sins.

Through the sacrifice that Jesus Christ made on your behalf, you have the opportunity to be saved from the guilt of your sins.

'Christ died for our sins'
(1 Corinthians chapter 15 verse 3 - KJV)

Sin

What is a sin?

A sin is any action or behavior or thought that fails to meet the standard of perfection established by God.

It is not possible for humans to meet the standards of perfection established by God.

Which means that I am a sinner, and so are you.

Even the most respectable among us, even the most high and mighty are sinners; even if you asked the Queen of England, she would admit that she is a sinner.

Sin is an unavoidable human condition.

We can't help it: we all sin, whether by thought or word or action, we all fall short of the standard of perfection established by God.

'All have sinned and fall short of the glory of God'
(Romans chapter 3 verse 23 - NIV)

Perhaps you think that you are safe because you haven't actually committed a sin recently; perhaps a married man looks at an attractive woman and thinks to himself how nice it would be to lie with her: But this is also sin.

Just thinking about sinning, is a sin.

Jesus said that, *"anyone who looks at a woman lustfully has already committed adultery with her in his heart."*
(Matthew chapter 5 verse 28 - NIV)

We are all sinners.

'If we claim to be without sin, we deceive ourselves and the truth is not in us.' (1 John chapter 1 verse 8 - NIV)

I think I've made it clear: you, me, and everyone else is a sinner, without exception.

How can you make yourself acceptable to God?

'If we confess our sins, he [God] is faithful and just and will forgive us our sins and purify us from all unrighteousness.'
(1 John chapter 1 verse 9 - NIV)

Realize that you are a sinner,
And ask God to forgive your sins.

God will forgive your sins, and his forgiveness will make you acceptable to God.

The reason why God can forgive you is because a sacrifice has been made on your behalf, a sacrifice so great that it has compensated God for all of your sins.
The perfect sacrifice was Jesus Christ.
Because of the crucifixion of Jesus Christ, you can receive forgiveness of your sins.

"I want you to know that through Jesus the forgiveness of sins is proclaimed to you. Through him everyone who believes is set free from every sin"
(Acts chapter 13 verses 38 and 39 - NIV)

Unlikely Heroes

God is the most important person, ever.

God is the creator of everything; he has existed forever and he will continue to exist forever.

God is all-powerful, all-knowing, and all-important.

There has never been, nor will there ever be anyone more important than God.

It would be natural to think that someone so supremely important as the Lord God Almighty would only choose the most important, most educated, most confident people to act and speak on his behalf. This would make a lot of sense to you and me.

However, as you read the Bible you realize that over and over again, God selects the least confident, the least socially acceptable, and the least among many to work for him; and God expects these unremarkable people to perform some of the most important tasks on his behalf.

Age is not a barrier to being useful to God: **Abraham** was 100 years old, and his wife **Sarah** was 90 years old when God gave them a son, making Abraham the father of a great nation. (Genesis chapter 21 verse 5)

Joseph was spoilt by his father, and he was abused by his jealous brothers. Joseph's brothers conspired to kill him, but changed their mind and sold him into slavery. Despite this, Joseph prospered in his new home in Egypt, and he was essential in God's plan for the survival of the Israelites. (Genesis chapter 37 verse 18)

Being adopted was not a disadvantage for **Moses**. (Exodus chapter 2 verse 10)
And Moses was not a confident speaker, claiming to be slow of speech and tongue, reasoning with God that he couldn't lead the people, or speak on God's behalf to the king of Egypt; but God used Moses to deliver his messages and lead his people out of slavery, all the way to the edge of the Promised Land. (Exodus chapter 4 verse 10)

Rahab was a prostitute, but she was very important in God's plan for the capture of the city of Jericho, which resulted in God's chosen people inheriting the Promised Land. (Joshua chapter 2)

King Saul ridiculed **David** because he was just a young boy, the youngest of eight brothers. David had offered to go and fight the enemy's giant warrior, Goliath; despite Saul's doubts, David killed Goliath and became a great king of Israel. (1 Samuel chapter 17 verse 33)

Paul was chosen by God to be an apostle and a very important educator in the early church. But Paul had been an enemy of Christians, actively hunting and persecuting them; Paul even admits to standing by and approving the stoning to death of an active Christian called Stephen. (Acts chapter 22 verse 20)

There are lots of examples of God using the least likely people to say and do important things on his behalf.
You don't need to be a clever or well-educated person.
You don't need to have a deep theological understanding of the Bible.
You don't need to be an highly respected citizen of the

community or an upstanding leader in a church organization.

As you read your Bible, you will discover many ordinary, timid, uneducated, and socially-unacceptable people whom God chose to do things on his behalf. And you should realize that if those people were important to God, you are also important to God: you can also be part of God's plan.

'It's in Christ that we find out who we are and what we are living for. Long before we first heard of Christ and got our hopes up, he had his eye on us, had designs on us for glorious living, part of the overall purpose he is working out in everything and everyone.'
(Ephesians chapter 1 verses 11 and 12 - MSG)

Here is something else to think about: -

When the Son of God came to earth and was born in human form as Jesus, he was not born into a palace; Jesus was born into the most humble and particularly vulnerable circumstances; and he was adopted by a carpenter tradesman who was pledged in marriage to Jesus' mother.

And when Jesus Christ was recruiting his disciples, he didn't go to the temple to select the respectable and knowledgeable leaders: Jesus Christ chose ordinary unremarkable people, like you and me.

'Brothers and sisters, think of what you were when you were called. Not many of you were wise by human standards; not many were influential; not many were of noble birth. But God chose the foolish things of the world to

shame the wise; God chose the weak things of the world to shame the strong. God chose the lowly things of this world and the despised things—and the things that are not—to nullify the things that are, so that no one may boast before him. It is because of him that you are in Christ Jesus, who has become for us wisdom from God—that is, our right-eousness, holiness and redemption. Therefore, as it is written: "Let the one who boasts boast in the Lord."
(1 Corinthians chapter 1 from verse 26 - NIV)

'I urge you, brothers and sisters, in view of God's mercy, to offer your bodies as a living sacrifice, holy and pleasing to God—this is your true and proper worship.'
(Romans chapter 12 verse 1 - NIV)

You may not feel special or important, but as a Christian it is very possible that God may already have a plan that requires your assistance. It might be something big, or it might be something small; but whatever it is, if it is God's plan, it will be important, because you are important to God.

Let the Holy Spirit guide your lives

Galatians 5:16 - NLT

O LORD, you have examined my heart
and know everything about me

Psalm 139:1 - NLT

End Note

I do not claim to possess any superior knowledge of the Bible. I am just a simple son of Ulster who wants to help you to understand the good message that God has for you.

I thank God that he has enabled me to be a small instrument in his service; and if the effort of producing this little book results in any one person accepting Jesus Christ as their Savior, it is to God that all of the praise and glory belongs.

Right at the end of the Bible, John gives a very stern warning: *'If anyone adds anything to what is written here, God will add to that person the plagues described in this book. And if anyone removes any of the words from this book of prophecy, God will remove that person's share in the tree of life and in the holy city that are described in this book.'* (Revelation 22 : 18, 19 - NLT)

I take John's warning very seriously. For this reason, if you find error or ambiguity in anything that I have attempted to explain, please get in touch through the publisher so that corrections can be considered for subsequent editions.

The grace of the Lord Jesus Christ be with you all. Amen
Revelation 22:21

Printed in Great Britain
by Amazon